Reading STREET

Grades **K-2**

Scott Foresman

Fluency
Teacher's Guide and Student Worktext

PEARSON

Glenview, Illinois
Boston, Massachusetts
Chandler, Arizona
Upper Saddle River, New Jersey

ISBN-13: 978-0-328-47746-3
ISBN-10:   0-328-47746-X
9 10 V016 18 17 16 15 14 13

Reading Street Response to Intervention Kit

Program Overview

The *Reading Street Response to Intervention Kit* provides targeted instruction in core English-Language Arts standards for Grades K to 2 in each of the five critical areas of reading instruction: phonemic awareness, phonics and decoding, fluency, vocabulary, and comprehension. The Kit, designed for small-group or one-on-one instruction, includes lessons on core skills, allowing teachers to focus on the skills children need most and to help them make rapid progress to achieve grade-level proficiency. For additional information about the *Reading Street Response to Intervention Kit*, see "How to Use This Kit" in the RTI Kit Implementation Guide.

Fluency Teacher's Guide and Student Worktext

The Teacher's Guide portion includes
- three-tiered, differentiated lessons
- specific guidance on how to measure fluency
- reinforcement for the strategies and routines used in the core program
- three customized mini-lessons differentiated for the following reading and skill levels:

> Odd-numbered lessons focus on these Words Correct Per Minute:
> > Mini-lesson 1: Level 1 (Model reading and do choral readings)
> > Mini-lesson 2: Level 2 (20–35 WCPM)
> > Mini-lesson 3: Level 3 (35–50 WCPM)
>
> Even-numbered lessons focus on these Words Correct Per Minute:
> > Mini-lesson 1: Level 1 (50–65 WCPM)
> > Mini-lesson 2: Level 2 (65–80 WCPM)
> > Mini-lesson 3: Level 3 (80–95 WCPM)

The Student Worktext portion includes
- additional reading opportunities
- additional skills practice
- School+Home activities on every page

Lesson Features
- **Set the scene** introduces the lesson topic to children.
- **Objectives** identify the instructional objectives for children.
- **Materials** list the Worktext components and additional supporting materials for the lesson, such as the Leveled Reader Database.
- **Direct teaching** is provided through explicit teacher modeling and consistent routines.
- **Mini-lessons** for differentiated instruction.
- **Guided practice** for each mini-lesson consists of ample group practice with multiple response opportunities.
- **Independent practice (On Their Own)** allows children to read independently, with a partner, or with a small group.
- **If.../then...** provides teachers with specific activities for reinforcing skills.

Table of Contents
Fluency

Readability in *Reading Street Response to Intervention Kit*

Children's reading levels in a single classroom often range greatly. In the Fluency Teacher's Guide and Student Worktext, mini-lessons and the corresponding Worktext reading passages are differentiated to cover a range of reading levels.

Odd-numbered Lessons

Mini-lesson 1: Level 1 (Model reading and do choral readings)

The short reading passages in the Worktext range from 40 to 65 words. The passages are comprised of the first 100 sight words and the most common nouns children will encounter in texts.

Mini-lesson 2: Level 2 (20–35 WCPM)

The Worktext reading passages have a readability index of 1.5 to 1.9. The passages range from 65 to 90 words and include basic sight words.

Mini-lesson 3: Level 3 (35–50 WCPM)

Reading passages have a readability index of 1.5 to 2.9 and range from 80 to 120 words.

Even-numbered Lessons

Mini-lesson 1: Level 1 (50–65 WCPM)

Reading passages range from 95 to 140 words and focus mainly on sight words and the most common nouns children will encounter in texts.

Mini-lesson 2: Level 2 (65–80 WCPM)

The Worktext reading passages have a readability index of 1.5 to 1.9. Reading passages range from 140 to 180 words.

Mini-lesson 3: Level 3 (80–95 WCPM)

Reading passages have a readability index of 1.5 to 2.9. Reading passages range from 160 to 215 words.

How to Measure Fluency

Use this routine with children when they are capable of doing timed self-assessments. Remind children that good readers read without mistake, with expression, and at a natural speed—as if they are speaking. Emphasize that learning to read this way takes practice and that keeping track of reading times helps children see how their reading improves with practice.

1. Introduce Timed Reading

Tell children that today they will read a story, such as "Car Wash" on Worktext p. 21, and keep track of how many words they read correctly in one minute. Explain that the numbers on the right side of the story are a running total of the words in the story.

Tell children that you will set a timer for one minute. They will underline any words they don't know as they read. When the timer goes off, children will draw a line after the last word they read.

2. Complete the First Timed Reading

Emphasize to children that timing their reading is not a race. The most important thing is to understand what they read. Encourage children to read the best they can. Tell children that they will start reading when you say "Begin."

Choose a passage that is neither too short nor too long, such as "Car Wash" on Worktext p. 21. Set the timer for one minute and have children whisper read the passage, marking it as you've instructed. Provide encouragement and prompting as needed.

3. Do the Numbers

After one minute, tell children that it's time to figure out how many words they read correctly. Show them how to use the words at the right of the story to identify the total number of words they read. Then have them count the words they underlined.

To figure out how many words they read correctly, tell children to take the total number of words they read and subtract the number of underlined words. For example, if their total is 65 words and they underlined 5 words, they will subtract 5 from 65. That would mean they read 60 words correct per minute (60 WCPM).

4. Track Progress

Distribute the Fluency Progress Chart from p. T•9. Tell children that they will use the chart to keep track of how many words they read correctly in one minute. Explain that the numbers on the left show the number of words they read correctly. The numbers on the bottom show how many times the children checked their reading. When children check their reading the first time, they will fill in the column that has a 1 at the bottom.

For example, if children read 60 words right, they will find the number 60 in the very first column and draw a line. Then they will color in everything in that column under that line. Use a colored pencil to demonstrate. Help children calculate and chart the number of words they read correctly for the first timed reading.

5. Practice On Their Own

Before pairing children for practice, review each child's underlined words. Point out familiar sound-spellings or word parts to help children read the words, or identify unfamiliar words and their meanings for them.

Explain to children that they will read the passage several times, and then they will do another timed reading to find out how much their reading has improved. Work with children to set new WCPM goals for the second timed reading. Use goals that correspond to the child's grade level goals.

Then pair children for practice. Have them take turns reading the story to each other three or four times. Tell partners to help each other with word identification and to encourage one another to read with expression.

6. Complete the Second Timed Reading

After sufficient practice, repeat the one-minute timed reading with the same passage. Have partners work together to figure out their words correct per minute (WCPM) and fill in their charts for their second timed reading. Have them determine if they reached the goal they set.

Name

Fluency Progress Chart

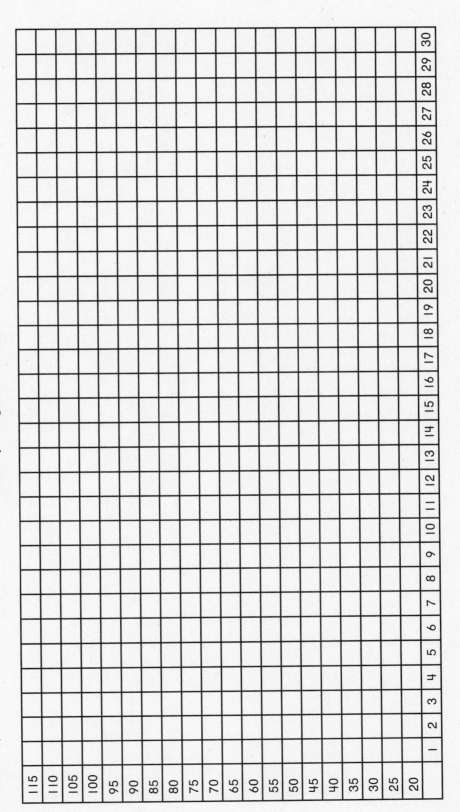

	1	2	3	4	5	6	7	8	9	10	11	12	13	14	15	16	17	18	19	20	21	22	23	24	25	26	27	28	29	30
115																														
110																														
105																														
100																														
95																														
90																														
85																														
80																														
75																														
70																														
65																														
60																														
55																														
50																														
45																														
40																														
35																														
30																														
25																														
20																														

Fluency Teacher's Guide

Fluency Lesson 1
Accuracy 1

Objectives:
- Read fluently without errors, making sure to read each word and read it correctly.

MATERIALS

Worktext pp. 2–7
Routine Card 2
Leveled Reader Database

Set the scene Have children each name something they do well, such as playing soccer, playing video games, or setting the table. How did you get good at that? I bet you practiced. Tell children that to read well, they also have to practice. Good readers can read all the words correctly. Today we're going to practice reading because the more we practice, the better we'll get.

Model and teach Explain to children that today they'll read a story called "At Bat" on Worktext p. 2. We'll read all the words correctly and not skip over or change any words. Point out the periods and question marks. A period means that you're at the end of the sentence, so you stop for just a moment. A question mark means you're at the end of a question. You need to make your voice go up at the end so that you sound like you're asking a question.

- I will read the first two sentences aloud. I want to read without making any mistakes. I will stop for a moment when I get to a period. When I get to a question mark, I'll read it like I'm asking a question.
- Before I read aloud, I will take a moment to read the sentences to myself. This helps me become familiar with the words. Pause to read to yourself. Then have children follow along as you model reading the first two sentences with no mistakes.

Check Comprehension Who is batting? (Pig)

Mini-Lesson 1

Remind children that...
- they should read every word in the passage and read words correctly.
- they should pause when they see a period.
- a question mark shows that a question is being asked.

Guide Practice

Continue modeling accuracy by reading the rest of "At Bat" on Worktext p. 2 with no mistakes. Point to each word as you read it aloud. Then prepare students to read aloud the story with you. Give children time to read every two sentences silently before reading them aloud with you.

If... children cannot read a word,
then... have them blend decodable words (Routine Card 2).

On Their Own Prepare the group for a choral reading of "At Bat." Remember to read every word. Try to read all the words correctly. When you see a period, pause for a moment.

Routine	Choral Reading
1. Read Together	Have children read aloud with you.
2. Reread	Then have children read aloud without you. For optimal fluency, children should reread three or four times.
3. Provide Feedback	Listen to children and provide corrective feedback. Point out any words children read incorrectly.

Provide additional practice by assigning "Pets on Jets" on Worktext p. 3.

Mini-Lesson 2

Fluency Goal: 20–35 words correct per minute

Remind children that...
- they should read every word accurately and not skip over words.
- they should pause when they see a period.
- a sentence sometimes continues onto the next line.

Guide Practice

Remind children to pay attention to periods. Sometimes there is no period when you come to the end of a line. This means that the sentence continues onto the next line. Move your eyes quickly down to the beginning of the next line and continue to read without pausing.

Read aloud "Six Big Frogs" on Worktext p. 4 with children.

If... children have difficulty reading with accuracy, **then...** have them point to problem words and read them first with you and then without you.

On Their Own Pair children to do an oral reading of "Six Big Frogs."

Routine	Paired Reading
1. Reader 1 Begins	Reader 1 reads the story to Reader 2.
2. Reader 2 Begins	Reader 2 reads the story to Reader 1.
3. Reread	For optimal fluency, children should reread three to four times.
4. Provide Feedback	Listen to children read and provide corrective feedback. Point out any words children skip over or read incorrectly.

For additional practice, assign "Jen the Vet" on Worktext p. 5.

Mini-Lesson 3

Fluency Goal: 35–50 words correct per minute

Remind children that...
- they should read every word accurately and not skip over or substitute words.
- commas require a brief pause and end marks require a longer pause.
- quotation marks indicate words characters say.

Guide Practice

Review quotation marks and commas for children. There are quotation marks at the beginning and end of some groups of words. These are words that the story characters say. When you come to a comma, pause for just a brief moment before you continue reading.

Read the first two sentences of "Luke and Jack See Granddad" on Worktext p. 6 with children.

If... children substitute a word,

then... point to the misidentified word, sound it out, and read it correctly. Then model the sentence and have children repeat it after you.

On Their Own Pair children to do an oral reading of "Luke and Jack See Granddad."

Routine	Paired Reading
1. Reader 1 Begins	Reader 1 reads the story to Reader 2.
2. Reader 2 Begins	Reader 2 reads the story to Reader 1.
3. Reread	For optimal fluency, children should reread three to four times.
4. Provide Feedback	Listen to children read and provide corrective feedback regarding their fluency and their decoding.

For additional practice, use "Helping Hope Shop" on Worktext p. 7.

Fluency Lesson 2
Accuracy 2

Objectives:
- Read fluently without errors, making sure to read each word and read it correctly.

MATERIALS
Worktext pp. 8–13
Routine Card 2
Leveled Reader Database

Set the scene Tell children that they've been practicing skills to make them better readers. Explain that in today's lesson they're going to practice reading without making any mistakes. They will read all the words correctly and not skip over or change any words. Remember that the more we practice, the better we get.

Model and teach Explain to children that today they'll read a story called "The Fox and the Crow" on Worktext p. 8. When we finish reading the story, I will ask you some questions. Review periods and question marks for children who have not received this instruction in earlier lessons. Sometimes there is no punctuation when you come to the end of a line. This means that the sentence continues on the next line. Move your eyes quickly down to the beginning of the next line and continue to read without pausing.

- I will read the first two sentences aloud. I want to read without skipping over words or changing words. If there is no punctuation at the end of a line, I will look quickly down to the beginning of the next line and continue reading without pausing.
- Before I read aloud, I will take a moment to read the sentences to myself. This helps me become familiar with the words. Pause to read to yourself.

Have children follow along as you model reading the first two sentences with no mistakes in a way that sounds like natural speech. Model how to read a turnover sentence.

Check Comprehension What does Fox want to get from Crow? (a piece of bread)

Mini-Lesson 1

Fluency Goal: 50–65 words correct per minute
Remind children that...
- they should read every word in the passage and read words correctly.
- they should show excitement or surprise when they see an exclamation mark.
- quotation marks indicate that a character is speaking.

Guide Practice
Continue modeling accuracy by reading the rest of "The Fox and the Crow" on Worktext p. 8 with no mistakes. Point to each word as you read it aloud. Then prepare students to read aloud the story with you.

If... children cannot read a word,
then... have them blend decodable words **(Routine Card 2)**.

On Their Own Prepare the group for a choral reading of "The Fox and the Crow." Remember to read every word. Try to read all the words correctly. When you see a period, pause for a moment.

Routine	Choral Reading
1. Read Together	Have children read aloud with you.
2. Reread	Then have children read aloud without you. For optimal fluency, children should reread three or four times.
3. Provide Feedback	Listen to children and provide corrective feedback.

For additional practice, assign "School Bus" on Worktext p. 9.

Mini-Lesson 2

Fluency Goal: 65–80 words correct per minute
Remind children that...

- they should read every word accurately and not skip over words.
- they should pause when they see a period.
- a sentence sometimes continues onto the next line.

Guide Practice

Remind children that reading sentences silently will help them become familiar with the words. When we read silently to ourselves, we learn the words we will read aloud. Read the first two sentences silently. Give them a few moments to read the sentences silently.

Read aloud "The Loose Tooth" on Worktext p. 10 with children before having them do the paired reading in On Their Own.

If... children substitute a word,

then... point to the word, sound it out, and read it correctly. Then model the sentence and have children repeat it after you.

On Their Own Pair children to do an oral reading of "The Loose Tooth."

Routine	Paired Reading
1. Reader 1 Begins	Reader 1 reads the story to Reader 2.
2. Reader 2 Begins	Reader 2 reads the story to Reader 1.
3. Reread	For optimal fluency, children should reread three to four times. Listen to children read and provide corrective feedback. Point out any words children skip over or read incorrectly.
4. Provide Feedback	

For additional practice, assign "Ant Farm" on Worktext p. 11 with a partner.

Mini-Lesson 3

Fluency Goal: 80–95 words correct per minute
Remind children that...

- they should read every word accurately and not skip over or substitute words.
- they should read the story silently first to become familiar with the words.
- commas require a brief pause and end marks require a longer pause.

Guide Practice

Write the following words: *Leah, harvests,* and *gathers* from "Leah's Farm" on Worktext p. 12. Point to each word as you read it aloud. Then have children read the words with you and without you. Before having children read the first paragraph aloud, give them a few moments to read the paragraph silently.

If... children cannot accurately pronounce all of the words in the story,

then... model reading each difficult word two or three times and have children repeat after you. Repeat until children can read all words accurately.

On Their Own Pair children to do an oral reading of "Leah's Farm."

Routine	Paired Reading
1. Reader 1 Begins	Reader 1 reads the story to Reader 2.
2. Reader 2 Begins	Reader 2 reads the story to Reader 1.
3. Reread	For optimal fluency, children should reread three to four times. Listen to children read and provide corrective feedback regarding their fluency and their decoding.
4. Provide Feedback	

For additional practice, use "Nick's Trains" on Worktext p. 13.

Fluency Lesson 3
Rate 1

Objectives:
- Read fluently at the same speed as if you were speaking.

MATERIALS
Worktext pp. 14–19
Routine Cards 2, 8
Leveled Reader Database

Set the scene Explain to children that they've practiced reading a story so that they could read it without any mistakes. Today they will practice reading at the same speed they use when they are speaking to someone. When we read, we want to sound as if we are talking. After we have practiced reading the story, I will ask you some questions about what we read. You will see that by practicing, you can become a better reader.

Model and teach Explain that today children will read a story called "Little Sister" on Worktext p. 14. Explain that when they are finished, you will ask them to tell you about what they read.

Tell children that there are question marks at the end of some of the sentences. This means that those sentences ask questions. When you ask a question or read a question aloud, you make your voice go up at the end of the sentence.

- I will read the first three sentences aloud. I want to read so that it sounds as if I am talking to a friend. When I get to a question mark, I will make my voice go up at the end of the sentence.
- Before I read aloud, I will take a moment to read the sentences to myself. This helps me become familiar with the words. Pause to read to yourself.

Then have children follow along as you model reading the first three sentences at an appropriate rate.

Check Comprehension What color are Eva's eyes? (blue)

Mini-Lesson 1

Remind children that...
- they should read every word in the passage and read words correctly.
- they should read the sentences to themselves to become familiar with the words.
- their voice should go up when they see a question mark.

Guide Practice
Continue modeling rate by reading the rest of "Little Sister" on Worktext p. 14 at an appropriate rate. Point to each word as you read it aloud. Then prepare students to read aloud the story with you.

If... children cannot read a word,
then... have them blend decodable words
(Routine Card 2) or say and spell high-frequency words
(Routine Card 8).

On Their Own Prepare the group for a choral reading of "Little Sister." Remember to read every word. Try to read at the same speed that you normally speak. When you see a question mark, make your voice go up.

Routine	Choral Reading
1. Read Together	Have children read aloud with you.
2. Reread	Then have children read aloud without you. For optimal fluency, children should reread three or four times.
3. Provide Feedback	Listen to children and provide corrective feedback.

For additional practice, assign "Paul and the Red Ball" on Worktext p. 15.

Mini-Lesson 2

Fluency Goal: 20–35 words correct per minute

Remind children that…

- good readers should read at the same rate that they normally speak.
- they should use their voice to show excitement when they see an exclamation mark.
- a sentence sometimes continues onto the next line.

Guide Practice

Remind children to pay attention to the ends of sentences. When you see a period, pause before beginning to read the next sentence. When you see an exclamation point, use your voice to show excitement or surprise.

Read aloud "Duck Pond" on Worktext p. 16 with children before having them do the paired reading in On Their Own.

If… children cannot read fluently without you,

then… have them finish reading the story with you before reading it with partners.

On Their Own Pair children to do an oral reading of "Duck Pond."

Routine	Paired Reading
1. Reader 1 Begins	Reader 1 reads the story to Reader 2.
2. Reader 2 Begins	Reader 2 reads the story to Reader 1.
3. Reread	For optimal fluency, children should reread three to four times.
4. Provide Feedback	Listen to children read and provide corrective feedback. Point out if children read too fast or too slow.

Provide additional practice by having children read "Petting Zoo" on Worktext p. 17 with a partner.

Mini-Lesson 3

Fluency Goal: 35–50 words correct per minute

Remind children that…

- they should read at the same speed that they would speak.
- commas require a brief pause and end marks require a longer pause.
- quotation marks indicate words characters say.

Guide Practice

Review the use of quotation marks with children. There are quotation marks around some groups of words. These are words a character is saying. When we read a character's words, we try to talk the way we think the character would talk.

Read the first two sentences of "Dean's Neat Green Cast" on Worktext p. 18 with children.

If… children have difficulty reading as if they were talking with someone,

then… model reading a group of sentences and have children read the sentences with you.

On Their Own Pair children to do an oral reading of "Dean's Neat Green Cast."

Routine	Paired Reading
1. Reader 1 Begins	Reader 1 reads the story to Reader 2.
2. Reader 2 Begins	Reader 2 reads the story to Reader 1.
3. Reread	For optimal fluency, children should reread three to four times.
4. Provide Feedback	Listen to children read and provide corrective feedback regarding their fluency and their decoding.

For additional practice, use "Emma Learns to Skate" on Worktext p. 19.

Fluency Lesson 4
Rate 2

Objectives:
- Read as if you were speaking.

MATERIALS
Worktext pp. 20–25
Routine Cards 2, 8
Leveled Reader Database

Set the scene Call on several children to demonstrate how they walked in pairs on a recent school trip or class activity. Because no one walked too fast or too slow, we enjoyed our trip (or activity). Explain that when we read, it's helpful not to read too fast or too slow either. Instead of rushing through your reading, or reading very slowly, it's best to read as if you are talking to someone. We will practice reading this way in today's lesson.

Model and teach Explain to children that today they'll read a story called "A New Garden" on Worktext p. 20. When you are finished reading, I will ask you a question about the story.

Tell children to notice that there is a period at the end of each sentence. When they come to a period, they should stop for just a moment before they continue reading. A period means that you're at the end of the sentence, so you stop for just a moment before you continue reading.

- Before I read aloud, I will read the sentences to myself to help me become familiar with the words. Pause to read to yourself.
- As I read, I will stop for a moment when I come to a period. I will read as if I were talking to you.

Have children follow along as you model reading the first paragraph without any mistakes and at a pace that children will recognize as natural speech.

Check Comprehension What are Taye and Nita doing in the story? (planting a new garden in the park)

Mini-Lesson 1

Fluency Goal: 50–65 words correct per minute
Remind children that...
- they should read every word in the passage and read words correctly.
- they should pause when they see a period.
- a question mark shows that a question is being asked.

Guide Practice
Write the following words from "A New Garden" on Worktext p. 20: *Taye, Nita, beautiful,* and *flowers.* Point to each word as you read it aloud. Then have children read the words with you and without you. Then have children read the next paragraph aloud with you.

If... children cannot read a word,
then... have them blend decodable words (Routine Card 2) or say and spell high-frequency words (Routine Card 8).

On Their Own Prepare the group for a choral reading of "A New Garden." You are going to read the story aloud as a group. Do your best reading and try to read as if you were speaking to someone.

Routine	Choral Reading
1. Read Together	Have children read aloud with you.
2. Reread	Then have children read aloud without you. For optimal fluency, children should reread three or four times.
3. Provide Feedback	Listen to children and provide corrective feedback.

For additional practice, use "Car Wash" on Worktext p. 21.

Mini-Lesson 2

Fluency Goal: 65–80 words correct per minute

Remind children that...
- they should read at the same speed that they speak.
- they should pause for just a moment when they come to a comma.
- they should take a moment to read sentences to themselves before reading aloud.

Guide Practice

Write the following words from "At the Circus" on Worktext p. 22: *circus, Alonso, Carlos, elephants, proudly,* and *cheers*. Point to each word as you read it aloud. Then have children read the words with you and without you. Have children read the story aloud with you.

If... children read too slowly,

then... model a sentence or paragraph at a moderate rate and ask them to read it after you several times, each time reading a bit faster, until children have achieved a normal rate.

On Their Own Pair children to do an oral reading of "At the Circus."

Routine	Paired Reading
1. Reader 1 Begins	Reader 1 reads the story to Reader 2.
2. Reader 2 Begins	Reader 2 reads the story to Reader 1.
3. Reread	For optimal fluency, children should reread three to four times.
4. Provide Feedback	Listen to children read and provide corrective feedback. Point out any words children skip over or read incorrectly.

For additional practice, assign "Grocery Shopping" on Worktext p. 23.

Mini-Lesson 3

Fluency Goal: 80–95 words correct per minute

Remind children that...
- they should read at the same speed that they would speak.
- they should make words in capital letters stand out with their voices.
- they should show strong feeling when they read sentences ending with exclamation points.

Guide Practice

Write the following words from "The Middle of Nowhere" on Worktext p. 24: *understood, hiking, tracks,* and *forest.* Point to each word as you read it aloud. Then have children read the words with you and without you. Before having children read the story with you, give them a few moments to read the paragraphs silently.

If... children are reading too quickly,

then... model a sentence and ask them to track the print as they echo you, pointing to each word as they read it to help slow them down.

On Their Own Pair children to do an oral reading of "The Middle of Nowhere."

Routine	Paired Reading
1. Reader 1 Begins	Reader 1 reads the story to Reader 2.
2. Reader 2 Begins	Reader 2 reads the story to Reader 1.
3. Reread	For optimal fluency, children should reread three to four times.
4. Provide Feedback	Listen to children read and provide corrective feedback regarding their fluency and their decoding.

For additional practice, use "Curt's Birthday" on Worktext p. 25.

Fluency Lesson 5
Accuracy and Rate 1

Objectives:
- Read fluently without errors at the same rate at which you would speak.

MATERIALS
Worktext pp. 26–31
Routine Cards 2, 8
Leveled Reader Database

Set the scene Explain that when you listen to someone read a story, you don't want the reader to rush or read too slowly. You want to understand each word, and you want each sentence to sound like the reader is talking to you. You have practiced reading carefully in a way that sounds like talking. Today we will practice those skills. As we read and reread today's story, you will find that you begin to read the words without mistakes and without going too fast or too slow.

Model and teach Today we'll read a story called "Hot Rod." Turn to Worktext p. 26 and tell children that a hot rod is a small car that is built for fun and racing. When we have finished, I will ask you a question about the story.

Explain that there are periods at the end of most sentences. A period tells us to stop for just a moment. When we see a period, we make our voices go down.

- I will read the first two sentences aloud. I want to read without making any mistakes. I want to make sure that I am not reading too fast or too slow. I will make my voice go down when I see a period.
- Before I read aloud, I will read the sentences to myself to become familiar with the words. Pause to read to yourself.

Have children follow along as you model reading the first two sentences with no mistakes in a way that sounds like natural speech. Make sure you pause appropriately for periods.

Check Comprehension How many friends get in the hot rod with Dan? (five)

 **Mini-Lesson 1**

Remind children that...
- they should read every word in the passage and read words correctly.
- they should read at the same speed that they would talk to a friend.
- when they see a period, they should make their voices go down.

Guide Practice
Continue reading "Hot Rod" on Worktext p. 26. Before having children read the next two sentences aloud with you, give them a few moments to read the sentences silently.

If... children cannot read a word,
then... have them blend decodable words **(Routine Card 2)** or say and spell high-frequency words **(Routine Card 8)**.

On Their Own Prepare the group for a choral reading of "Hot Rod." Remember to read every word and try to read all the words correctly. Speak at the same speed you would talk to a friend. When you see a period, make your voice go down. When you see a question mark, make your voice go up.

Routine	Choral Reading
1. Read Together	Have children read aloud with you.
2. Reread	Then have children read aloud without you. For optimal fluency, children should reread three or four times.
3. Provide Feedback	Listen to children and provide corrective feedback.

For additional practice, assign "On the Playground" on Worktext p. 27.

Mini-Lesson 2

Fluency Goal: 20–35 words correct per minute

Remind children that...

- they should read every word accurately and at the same speed that they normally talk.
- when they see an exclamation point, they should show surprise and excitement.
- sometimes a sentence continues onto the next line.

Guide Practice

Before having children read the first group of sentences aloud with you, give them a few moments to read the story silently. Then read aloud "Sand Fun" on Worktext p. 28 with children before having them do the paired reading in On Their Own.

If... children have difficulty reading with accuracy, **then...** have them point to problem words and read them first with you and then without you.

On Their Own Pair children to do an oral reading of "Sand Fun."

Routine	Paired Reading
1. Reader 1 Begins	Reader 1 reads the story to Reader 2.
2. Reader 2 Begins	Reader 2 reads the story to Reader 1.
3. Reread	For optimal fluency, children should reread three to four times.
4. Provide Feedback	Listen to children read and provide corrective feedback. Point out any words children skip over or read incorrectly.

Provide additional practice by having children read "At the Airport" on Worktext p. 29 with a partner.

Mini-Lesson 3

Fluency Goal: 35–50 words correct per minute

Remind children that...

- they should read every word accurately and not skip over or substitute words.
- they should read at the same speed they would speak to a friend.
- sometimes a sentence continues onto the next line.

Guide Practice

Explain to children that when there is no punctuation mark at the end of a line, they need to look down to the beginning of the next line and continue reading until they come to a punctuation mark. Have children follow along as you model reading the first group of sentences in "Jack's Trip" on Worktext p. 30. Then have children read the next group of sentences aloud with you.

If... children skip over words,

then... have them track the print as they practice and then have children read the story without tracking.

On Their Own Pair children to do an oral reading of "Jack's Trip."

Routine	Paired Reading
1. Reader 1 Begins	Reader 1 reads the story to Reader 2.
2. Reader 2 Begins	Reader 2 reads the story to Reader 1.
3. Reread	For optimal fluency, children should reread three to four times.
4. Provide Feedback	Listen to children read and provide corrective feedback regarding their fluency and their decoding.

For additional practice, use "Our Solar System" on Worktext p. 31.

Fluency Lesson 6
Accuracy and Rate 2

Objectives:
- Read fluently without errors at the same rate at which you would speak.

MATERIALS
Worktext pp. 32–37
Routine Cards 2, 8
Leveled Reader Database

Set the scene Explain that when we sing together, we don't sing too fast or too slow. The same thing happens when we read. We don't rush through a story or read it too slowly. Instead, we read as if we are talking to a friend. We will practice reading in this way in today's lesson. Practicing reading as if you are speaking to a friend will make you a better reader. After you finish reading the story, I will ask you a question about it.

Model and teach Tell children that today they'll read a story called "Bob's New Dog" on Worktext p. 32. Make sure children understand that a vet is a special doctor who takes care of animals.

Point out that there are commas between words in some sentences. Tell children that a comma signals a short pause before you continue to read.

- I will read the first paragraph aloud without making any mistakes. I will read in a way that sounds like I am talking to you.
- Before I read aloud, I will take a moment to read the paragraph to myself. This helps me become familiar with the words. Pause to read to yourself.

Have children follow along as you model reading the first paragraph with no mistakes and at a pace that children will recognize as natural speech.

Check Comprehension Why does Penny eat three times a day? (She is still growing.)

Mini-Lesson 1

Fluency Goal: 50–65 words correct per minute
Remind children that...
- they should read every word in the passage and read words correctly.
- they should read at the same speed that they would talk to a friend.
- when they see a comma, they should pause briefly.

Guide Practice
Write the following words from "Bob's New Dog" on Worktext p. 32: *Penny, bowls,* and *vet.* Point to each word as you read it aloud. Then have children read the words with you and without you. Then have children read the next paragraph aloud with you.

If... children cannot read a word,
then... have them blend decodable words **(Routine Card 2)** or say and spell high-frequency words **(Routine Card 8).**

On Their Own Prepare the group for a choral reading of "Bob's New Dog." Remember to read every word, and try to read all the words correctly. Speak at the same speed you would talk to someone.

Routine	Choral Reading
1. Read Together	Have children read aloud with you.
2. Reread	Then have children read aloud without you. For optimal fluency, children should reread three or four times.
3. Provide Feedback	Listen to children and provide corrective feedback. Point out if children read too fast or too slow.

Provide additional practice by assigning "Allie's Art" on Worktext p. 33.

Mini-Lesson 2

Fluency Goal: 65–80 words correct per minute
Remind children that...
- they should read every word accurately and at the same speed that they normally talk.
- they should make their voice go up when they see a question mark.
- sometimes a sentence continues onto the next line.

Guide Practice
Make sure children understand the words *hiss, purr,* and *meow* by having volunteers demonstrate the sounds. Then have children follow along as you model reading the first sentence of "Cats" on Worktext p. 34. Make sure you don't pause inappropriately when you read a turnover sentence. Read aloud "Cats!" with children before having them do the paired reading in On Their Own.

If... children have difficulty reading with accuracy, **then...** have them point to problem words and read them first with you and then without you.

On Their Own Pair children to do an oral reading of "Cats!"

Routine	Paired Reading
1. Reader 1 Begins	Reader 1 reads the story to Reader 2.
2. Reader 2 Begins	Reader 2 reads the story to Reader 1.
3. Reread	For optimal fluency, children should reread three to four times.
4. Provide Feedback	Listen to children read and provide corrective feedback. Point out any words children skip over or read incorrectly.

Provide additional practice by having children read "Baking Cookies" on Worktext p. 35 with a partner.

Mini-Lesson 3

Fluency Goal: 80–95 words correct per minute
Remind children that...
- they should read every word accurately and at a good pace.
- they should take a moment to read the paragraphs to themselves.
- they should show excitement or surprise when they see an exclamation mark.

Guide Practice
Explain that some sentences end with an exclamation mark. Tell children to read these sentences using a strong or excited voice to show strong feeling or excitement. Have children follow along as you model reading the first paragraph of "Moving Day" on Worktext p. 36. Then have children read the next paragraph with you.

If... children are reading too fast or too slow, **then...** model reading at a normal rate and ask them to echo read, each time reading a bit faster or slower, until children have achieved a moderate rate.

On Their Own Pair children to do an oral reading of "Moving Day."

Routine	Paired Reading
1. Reader 1 Begins	Reader 1 reads the story to Reader 2.
2. Reader 2 Begins	Reader 2 reads the story to Reader 1.
3. Reread	For optimal fluency, children should reread three to four times.
4. Provide Feedback	Listen to children read and provide corrective feedback regarding their fluency and their decoding.

For additional practice, use "Soccer Game" on Worktext p. 37.

Accuracy and Rate 3

Objectives:
- Read fluently without errors and at the same rate at which you would speak.

MATERIALS

Worktext pp. 38–43
Routine Cards 2, 8
Leveled Reader Database

Set the scene

When children read, advise them not to read too fast or too slow. Today they will practice those skills. Explain that the more they practice, the better their reading will become.

Model and teach

Today we'll read a story called "First Day of School." Turn to Worktext p. 38. When we have finished reading, I will ask you a question about the story.

Tell children that there are question marks at the end of some sentences. When you read a question aloud, you make your voice go up at the end of the sentence.

- I will read the first four sentences aloud. I want to read without making any mistakes. If the sentence ends with a question, I will read it like I am asking a question.
- Before I read aloud, I will take a moment to read the sentences to myself. This helps me become familiar with the words. Pause to read to yourself.

Have children follow along as you model reading the first four sentences with no mistakes in a way that sounds like natural speech.

Check Comprehension

Who walks Tim to school? (Mom)

Remind children that...
- they should read every word in the passage and read words correctly.
- they should read at the same speed that they would talk to a friend.
- they should make their voices go up when they see a question mark.

Guide Practice

Continue reading "First Day of School" on Worktext p. 38. Before having children read the next four sentences aloud with you, give them a few moments to read the sentences silently.

If... children cannot read a word,

then... have them blend decodable words **(Routine Card 2)** or say and spell high-frequency words **(Routine Card 8)**.

On Their Own Prepare the group for a choral reading of "First Day of School." You are going to read the story aloud as a group. Read carefully and try not to leave out or change any words. Read at a speed that sounds like talking.

Routine	Choral Reading
1. Read Together	Have children read aloud with you.
2. Reread	Then have children read aloud without you. For optimal fluency, children should reread three or four times.
3. Provide Feedback	Listen to children and provide corrective feedback.

For additional practice, assign "Yard Work" on Worktext p. 39.

Mini-Lesson 2

Fluency Goal: 20–35 words correct per minute
Remind children that...
- they should read every word accurately at the same speed that they normally talk.
- they should pause when they see a period at the end of a sentence.
- sometimes a sentence continues onto the next line.

Guide Practice
Have children follow along as you model reading the first two sentences of "Buddy" on Worktext p. 40 without pausing for turnover sentences. Before having children read the next group of sentences aloud, give them a few moments to read the sentences silently. Continue in this way for the remaining sentences.

If... children substitute a word,
then... point to the misidentified word, read it aloud, and have children repeat it. Then model the entire sentence and have them repeat until they read without errors.

On Their Own Pair children to do an oral reading of "Buddy."

Routine	Paired Reading
1. Reader 1 Begins	Reader 1 reads the story to Reader 2.
2. Reader 2 Begins	Reader 2 reads the story to Reader 1.
3. Reread	For optimal fluency, children should reread three to four times.
4. Provide Feedback	Listen to children read and provide corrective feedback. Point out any words children skip over or read incorrectly.

Provide additional practice by having children read "The Moon" on Worktext p. 41 with a partner.

Mini-Lesson 3

Fluency Goal: 35–50 words correct per minute
Remind children that...
- they should read every word accurately and at a good pace.
- commas signal a short pause in a sentence.
- quotation marks around words show that a character is speaking.

Guide Practice
Write the following words from "A New Friend" on Worktext p. 42: *didn't, can't, cross,* and *I'll.* Point to each word as you read it aloud. Then have children read the words with and without you. Before having children read the first paragraph with you, have them take a few moments to read the paragraph silently.

If... children skip over words,
then... have them track the print as they practice. Then have them read the story without tracking.

On Their Own Pair children to do an oral reading of "A New Friend."

Routine	Paired Reading
1. Reader 1 Begins	Reader 1 reads the story to Reader 2.
2. Reader 2 Begins	Reader 2 reads the story to Reader 1.
3. Reread	For optimal fluency, children should reread three to four times.
4. Provide Feedback	Listen to children read and provide corrective feedback regarding their fluency and their decoding.

For additional practice, use "Trucks" on Worktext p. 43.

Fluency Lesson 8
Accuracy and Rate 4

Objectives:
- Read fluently without errors at the same rate at which you would speak.

MATERIALS

Worktext pp. 44–49
Routine Cards 2, 8
Leveled Reader Database

Set the scene Explain to children that they have practiced reading all the words correctly without skipping over or changing them. Today they will continue to practice. We want to be careful not to read too fast or too slow, so we will also practice reading a story at the same speed we use when we talk to someone. Practicing will make you all better readers.

Model and teach Tell children that today they'll read a story called "Cool!" on Worktext p. 44. Make sure children know that dolphins are mammals that live in the ocean. They are very intelligent animals that can be trained to perform tricks. When we have finished reading, I will ask you a question about the story.

There are commas between some words in the sentences. When you come to a comma, pause for just a second before continuing to read.

Explain that you will read the first paragraph aloud and that you will try to read without making any mistakes and in a way that sounds like you are talking, not too fast or too slow. Before I read aloud, I will take a moment to read the sentences to myself. This helps me become familiar with the words. Pause to read to yourself. Have children follow along as you model reading the first paragraph with no mistakes in a way that sounds like natural speech.

Check Comprehension What leaped out of the water? (dolphins)

 **Mini-Lesson 1**

Fluency Goal: 50–65 words correct per minute
Remind children that...
- they should read every word in the passage and read words correctly.
- they should read at the same speed that they would talk to a friend.
- when they see a comma, they should pause briefly.

Guide Practice

Continue reading "Cool!" on Worktext p. 44. Before having children read the next paragraph aloud with you, give them a few moments to read the sentences silently. Continue in this way for the remaining sentences.

If... children cannot read a word,
then... have them blend decodable words
(Routine Card 2) or say and spell high-frequency words
(Routine Card 8).

On Their Own Prepare the group for a choral reading of "Cool!" You are going to read the story aloud as a group. Read carefully and don't leave out or change any words. Read at a speed that sounds like talking.

Routine	Choral Reading
1. Read Together	Have children read aloud with you.
2. Reread	Then have children read aloud without you. For optimal fluency, children should reread three or four times.
3. Provide Feedback	Listen to children and provide corrective feedback.

If children read the passage fluently, provide additional practice by assigning "The Pumpkin Patch" on Worktext p. 45.

Mini-Lesson 2

Fluency Goal: 65–80 words correct per minute

Remind children that…

- they should read every word accurately at the same speed that they normally talk.
- they should pause when they see a period at the end of a sentence.
- sometimes a sentence continues onto the next line.

Guide Practice

Write the following words from "Apples" on Worktext p. 46: *Gala, Honeycrisp,* and *themselves.* Point to each word as you read it out loud. Make sure children know that Gala and Honeycrisp are varieties of apples. Have children follow along as you model reading the first paragraph. Before having children read the next paragraph aloud, give them a few moments to read the sentences silently.

If… children are reading too fast or too slow, **then…** ask them to listen as you read at a normal pace.

Then have children echo your reading, first with you and then without you.

On Their Own Pair children to do an oral reading of "Apples."

Routine	Paired Reading
1. Reader 1 Begins	Reader 1 reads the story to Reader 2.
2. Reader 2 Begins	Reader 2 reads the story to Reader 1.
3. Reread	For optimal fluency, children should reread three to four times.
4. Provide Feedback	Listen to children read and provide corrective feedback. Point out any words children skip over or read incorrectly.

Assign "Swimming Lessons" on Worktext p. 47.

Mini-Lesson 3

Fluency Goal: 80–95 words correct per minute

Remind children that…

- they should read every word accurately and at a good pace.
- commas signal a short pause in a sentence.
- quotation marks around words show that a character is speaking.

Guide Practice

Have children follow along as you model reading the first paragraph of "A Room Full of Music" on Worktext p. 48. Before having children read the next paragraph with you, have them take a few moments to read the paragraph silently. There are quotation marks around groups of words that the characters say. We should read these words as we think the characters would say them.

If… children cannot read fluently without you,

then… have them finish reading the story with you before they read it in pairs.

On Their Own Pair children to do an oral reading of "A Room Full of Music."

Routine	Paired Reading
1. Reader 1 Begins	Reader 1 reads the story to Reader 2.
2. Reader 2 Begins	Reader 2 reads the story to Reader 1.
3. Reread	For optimal fluency, children should reread three to four times.
4. Provide Feedback	Listen to children read and provide corrective feedback regarding their fluency and their decoding.

For additional practice, use "Texas" on Worktext p. 49.

Fluency Lesson 9
Appropriate Phrasing/Punctuation Cues 1

Objectives:
- Attend to punctuation while reading, pausing in appropriate places.

MATERIALS

Worktext pp. 50–55
Routine Cards 2, 8
Leveled Reader Database

Set the scene Explain that today you will pay special attention to phrasing, or the way the words are grouped together in a sentence to give meaning. Children will practice pausing after commas and reading words together in groups instead of reading word-by-word.

Model and teach Tell children that today they'll read a story called "Monday Morning" on Worktext p. 50. After you have finished reading, I will ask you a question about what you read.

Explain that there are commas between some words in the sentences. Commas are clues that tell us to pause briefly. They also help us group words into phrases. Model how to read groups of words, such as the phrases "in the morning" and "by the way." Write the phrases on the board. First, read the phrases word-by-word. Then model how to read them correctly. Point out how reading words in groups helps readers understand the text better.

- Tell students you will read the first two sentences aloud. I will pause briefly after each comma and group words together as I read.
- Before I read aloud, I will read the sentences to myself. This helps me become familiar with the words. Pause to read to yourself.

Have children follow along as you model reading the first two sentences. Pay special attention to pausing at commas and grouping words appropriately.

Check Comprehension Where did Ruby open her book? (at her desk)

Mini-Lesson 1

Remind children that...
- they should read every word in the passage correctly and read at a normal pace.
- they should pause briefly when they see a comma.
- they should group words as they read.

Guide Practice
Continue reading "Monday Morning" on Worktext p. 50. Before having children read the next two sentences aloud with you, give them a few moments to read the sentences silently. Continue in this way for the remaining sentences.

If... children cannot read a word,
then... have them blend decodable words (Routine Card 2) or say and spell high-frequency words (Routine Card 8).

On Their Own Prepare the group for a choral reading of "Monday Morning." Explain that children are going to read the story aloud as a group. Remind them to read carefully and not leave out or change any words. Tell children to pause briefly when they see a comma and group words as they read.

Routine	Choral Reading
1. Read Together	Have children read aloud with you.
2. Reread	Then have children read aloud without you. For optimal fluency, children should reread three or four times.
3. Provide Feedback	Listen to children and provide corrective feedback.

Then assign "Robin's Nest" on Worktext p. 51.

Mini-Lesson 2

Fluency Goal: 20–35 words correct per minute
Remind children that...
- they should read every word accurately at the same speed that they normally talk.
- they should pause briefly when they see a comma.
- they should group words as they read.

Guide Practice
Have children follow along as you model reading the first two sentences of "Lake Cake" on Worktext p. 52, pausing briefly for commas and paying particular attention to grouping words. Before having children read the next two sentences aloud, give them a few moments to read the sentences silently.

If... children are not using punctuation cues correctly, **then...** write *Jake wants to fish, but Jake likes cake.* Ask them to point to the comma. Make sure each child understands that this is where to pause. Model the sentence and have children echo three or four times.

On Their Own Pair children to do an oral reading of "Lake Cake."

Routine	Paired Reading
1. Reader 1 Begins	Reader 1 reads the story to Reader 2.
2. Reader 2 Begins	Reader 2 reads the story to Reader 1.
3. Reread	For optimal fluency, children should reread three to four times.
4. Provide Feedback	Listen to children read and provide corrective feedback. Point out any words children skip over or read incorrectly.

Then have children read "Jenna's Bike" on Worktext p. 53 with a partner.

Mini-Lesson 3

Fluency Goal: 35–50 words correct per minute
Remind children that...
- they should read every word accurately and at a good pace.
- commas signal a short pause in a sentence.
- quotation marks around words show that a character is speaking.

Guide Practice
Explain that most sentences end with a period. It signals that children should come to a complete stop at the end of a sentence and pause longer than they would for a comma. Have children follow along as you model reading the first paragraph of "Andy and the Lion" on Worktext p. 54. Before having children read the next paragraph with you, have them take a few moments to read the paragraph silently.

If... children are having difficulty with phrasing, **then...** read selected text and group words together. Then read with appropriate phrasing and have children echo three or four times.

On Their Own Pair children to do an oral reading of "Andy and the Lion."

Routine	Paired Reading
1. Reader 1 Begins	Reader 1 reads the story to Reader 2.
2. Reader 2 Begins	Reader 2 reads the story to Reader 1.
3. Reread	For optimal fluency, children should reread three to four times.
4. Provide Feedback	Listen to children read and provide corrective feedback regarding their fluency and their decoding.

For additional practice, use "Snow Day" on Worktext p. 55.

Fluency Lesson 10
Appropriate Phrasing/Punctuation Cues 2

Objectives:
- Attend to punctuation while reading, pausing in appropriate places.

MATERIALS
Worktext pp. 56–61
Routine Cards 2, 8
Leveled Reader Database

Set the scene Explain to children that today they will work on reading with correct phrasing. During reading, children should think about reading phrases, or groups of words, together instead of just reading word-by-word. Explain that some sentences are long, so it's important to read words in groups that make sense. Grouping words into phrases can help children understand what they are reading.

Model and teach Tell children that today they'll read a story called "Luca's New Bike" on Worktext p. 56. After you have finished reading, I will ask you a question about what you read. There are commas in many of the sentences. They help us figure out how to divide the sentences into phrases as we read. You should pause briefly when you come to a comma.

- I will read the first paragraph aloud. I want to group the words as I read instead of reading word-by-word. When I get to a period, I will stop for a moment before I read the next sentence.
- Tell children that before you read aloud, you will take a moment to read the paragraph to yourself. Explain that this helps readers become familiar with the words and how they should read the phrases in the sentences. Pause to read to yourself.

Have children follow along as you model reading the first paragraph, paying special attention to appropriate phrasing.

Check Comprehension Why does Luca need money? (He wants to buy a bike.)

Fluency Goal: 50–65 words correct per minute
Remind children that...
- they should read every word in the passage correctly and read at a normal pace.
- when they see a comma, they should pause briefly.
- they should group words as they read.

Guide Practice
Continue reading "Luca's New Bike" on Worktext p. 56. Before having children read the next paragraph aloud with you, give them a few moments to read the paragraph silently. Continue in this way for the remaining paragraphs.

If... children cannot read a word,
then... have them blend decodable words (Routine Card 2) or say and spell high-frequency words (Routine Card 8).

On Their Own Prepare the group for a choral reading of "Luca's New Bike." You are going to read the story aloud as a group. Read carefully and don't leave out or change any words. Pause briefly when you see a comma and group words as you read.

Routine	Choral Reading
1. Read Together	Have children read aloud with you.
2. Reread	Then have children read aloud without you. For optimal fluency, children should reread three or four times.
3. Provide Feedback	Listen to children and provide corrective feedback.

Provide additional practice by assigning "Robots Explore the Ocean" on Worktext p. 57.

Mini-Lesson 2

Fluency Goal: 65–80 words correct per minute
Remind children that…
- they should read every word accurately at the same speed that they normally talk.
- they should pause briefly when they see a comma.
- some sentences continue on the next line.

Guide Practice

Have children follow along as you model reading the first paragraph of "Helping Grandfather" on Worktext p. 58, pausing briefly for commas and paying particular attention to grouping words. Before having children read the next two sentences aloud, give them a few moments to read the sentences silently.

If… children are pausing inappropriately within phrases, **then…** model appropriate phrasing and have children echo three or four times.

On Their Own Pair children to do an oral reading of "Helping Grandfather."

Routine	Paired Reading
1. Reader 1 Begins	Reader 1 reads the story to Reader 2.
2. Reader 2 Begins	Reader 2 reads the story to Reader 1.
3. Reread	For optimal fluency, children should reread three to four times.
4. Provide Feedback	Listen to children read and provide corrective feedback. Point out any words children skip over or read incorrectly.

Provide additional practice by having children read "Camping Trip" on Worktext p. 59 with a partner.

Mini-Lesson 3

Fluency Goal: 80–95 words correct per minute
Remind children that…
- they should read every word accurately and at a good pace.
- commas signal a short pause in a sentence.
- quotation marks around words show that a character is speaking.

Guide Practice

Have children follow along as you model reading the first paragraph of "A Big Game for Everyone!" on Worktext p. 60. Before having children read the next paragraph with you, have them take a few moments to read the paragraph silently. Tell children to pause for commas and group the words so they make sense.

If… children are having difficulty with phrasing where commas are present, **then…** make sure children can identify commas in selected text. Point out the commas if necessary. Model the text and have children echo three or four times.

On Their Own Pair children to do an oral reading of "A Big Game for Everyone!"

Routine	Paired Reading
1. Reader 1 Begins	Reader 1 reads the story to Reader 2.
2. Reader 2 Begins	Reader 2 reads the story to Reader 1.
3. Reread	For optimal fluency, children should reread three to four times.
4. Provide Feedback	Listen to children read and provide corrective feedback regarding their fluency and their decoding.

For additional practice, use "Dwayne's Birthday Surprise" on Worktext p. 61.

Appropriate Phrasing/Punctuation Cues 3

Objectives:
- Attend to punctuation while reading and group words into phrases.

MATERIALS
Worktext pp. 62–67
Routine Cards 2, 8
Leveled Reader Database

Set the scene Review punctuation and phrasing with children. We have learned how to pay attention to punctuation as we read. Today we will practice reading with correct phrasing. We will practice reading words together in groups so they make sense and are easy to understand. We'll pay careful attention to commas because they are clues about how to group words when we read.

Model and teach Introduce the reading passage "My Brother" on Worktext p. 62. After we have finished reading, I will ask you a question about what we read.
There are commas in some of the sentences. As a reader, you should pause briefly when you come to a comma.

- Tell children that you will read the first two sentences aloud and that as you read, you will group words together in phrases that make sense. I will not pause in the middle of a phrase. I will pause briefly when I come to a comma.
- Explain to children that before you read aloud, you will first read the sentences to yourself. This helps readers become familiar with the words. Pause to read to yourself.

Have children follow along as you model reading the first two sentences, paying special attention to correct phrasing.

Check Comprehension How does Roberto play with his brother? (by playing catch and going fishing)

Mini-Lesson 1

Remind children that...
- they should pause briefly for commas.
- they should group words into phrases that make sense.
- they should read every word in the passage correctly and at a normal pace.

Guide Practice
Write the following words from "My Brother" on Worktext p. 62: *friend, catch, fishing,* and *breakfast.* Point to each word as you read it aloud. Then have children read the words with you and then without you. Have children read the next two sentences aloud with you.

If... children cannot read a word,
then... have them blend decodable words
(Routine Card 2) or say and spell high-frequency words
(Routine Card 8).

On Their Own Prepare the group for a choral reading of "My Brother." Read carefully and don't leave out or change any words. Pause briefly when you see a comma and group words into phrases that make sense as you read.

Routine	Choral Reading
1. Read Together	Have children read aloud with you.
2. Reread	Then have children read aloud without you. For optimal fluency, children should reread three or four times.
3. Provide Feedback	Listen to children and provide corrective feedback.

Provide additional practice by assigning "Walking Dogs" on Worktext p. 63.

Mini-Lesson 2

Fluency Goal: 20–35 words correct per minute
Remind children that...

- when they see a comma, they should pause briefly.
- as they read, they should group words into phrases that make sense.
- they should read every word accurately at the same speed that they normally talk.

Guide Practice

Have children follow along as you model reading the first two sentences of "A Clean Room" on Worktext p. 64. Pause briefly for commas and pay particular attention to grouping words. Before having children read the next two sentences aloud, read aloud phrases from those sentences, such as "every morning" and "little sister."

If... children cannot read fluently without you,
then... have them finish reading the story with you before reading it with partners.

On Their Own Pair children to do an oral reading of "A Clean Room."

Routine	Paired Reading
1. Reader 1 Begins	Reader 1 reads the story to Reader 2.
2. Reader 2 Begins	Reader 2 reads the story to Reader 1.
3. Reread	For optimal fluency, children should reread three to four times.
4. Provide Feedback	Listen to children read and provide corrective feedback. Point out any phrases children read word-by-word.

Provide additional practice by having children read "Fire Drill" on Worktext p. 65 with a partner.

Mini-Lesson 3

Fluency Goal: 35–50 words correct per minute
Remind children that...

- commas signal a short pause in a sentence.
- they should group words into phrases that make sense.
- they should read every word accurately and at a good pace.

Guide Practice

Have children follow along as you model reading the first paragraph of "Fourth of July" on Worktext p. 66. First, read all words together and in a monotone voice. Then reread with appropriate phrasing. Discuss with children which reading was easier to understand and why. Before having children read the next paragraph with you, give them a few moments to read the paragraph silently.

If... children are having difficulty with phrasing,
then... model reading the first two sentences again with appropriate phrasing, and have children repeat after you.

On Their Own Pair children to do an oral reading of "Fourth of July."

Routine	Paired Reading
1. Reader 1 Begins	Reader 1 reads the story to Reader 2.
2. Reader 2 Begins	Reader 2 reads the story to Reader 1.
3. Reread	For optimal fluency, children should reread three to four times.
4. Provide Feedback	Listen to children read and provide corrective feedback regarding their fluency and their decoding.

For additional practice, use "Tigers" on Worktext p. 67.

Fluency Lesson 12
Appropriate Phrasing/Punctuation Cues 4

Objectives:
- Attend to punctuation while reading and group words into phrases.

MATERIALS
Worktext pp. 68–73
Routine Cards 2, 8
Leveled Reader Database

Set the scene
Review punctuation cues and phrasing with students. We have learned how to pay attention to punctuation as we read. Today we will practice reading with correct phrasing. Explain to children that when they read, they should read words together in groups so they make sense and are easy to understand. Encourage children to pay careful attention to commas because they are clues about how to group words.

Model and teach
Introduce the reading passage "The Street Fair" on Worktext p. 68. After you have finished reading, I will ask you a question about what you read.
Tell children that sometimes there will be no punctuation at the end of a line. This means that the sentence continues on the next line. Tell children to move their eyes quickly down to the beginning of the next line and read without pausing.
- I will read the first two sentences aloud. As I read, I will group words together in phrases that make sense. I will not pause in the middle of a phrase. I will pause briefly when I come to a comma and pause longer at a period. Where there is no punctuation at the end of a line, I will look down to the next line and read without pausing.
- Explain to children that before you read aloud, you will read the sentences to yourself to become familiar with the words. Pause to read to yourself.
Have children follow along as you model reading the first two sentences, paying special attention to punctuation and correct phrasing.

Check Comprehension
What do Eddie and Maya do after lunch? (sing and dance with their neighbors)

Fluency Goal: 50–60 words correct per minute
Remind children that...
- they should group words into phrases that make sense.
- they should read every word in the passage correctly and at a normal pace.
- sometimes a sentence continues onto the next line.

Guide Practice
Continue reading "The Street Fair" on Worktext p. 68 before having children read the next two sentences aloud with you, give them a few moments to read the sentences silently. Continue in this way for the remaining sentences.

If... children cannot read a word,
then... have them blend decodable words (**Routine Card 2**) or say and spell high-frequency words (**Routine Card 8**).

On Their Own Prepare the group for a choral reading of "The Street Fair." You are going to read the story aloud as a group. As you read, watch for commas and group together words into phrases that make sense as you read.

Routine	Choral Reading
1. Read Together	Have children read aloud with you.
2. Reread	Then have children read aloud without you. For optimal fluency, children should reread three or four times.
3. Provide Feedback	Listen to children and provide corrective feedback.

Provide additional practice by assigning "Amy's New Pet" on Worktext p. 69.

Mini-Lesson 2

Fluency Goal: 65–80 words correct per minute

Remind children that...

- they should group words into phrases that make sense as they read.
- they should read every word accurately at the same speed that they normally talk.
- they should show excitement or surprise when a sentence ends with an exclamation mark.

Guide Practice

Write the following words from "The Lion and the Mouse" on Worktext p. 70: *asleep, roar, net,* and *hunters.* Make sure children understand that a net can capture or hold something. Have children follow along as you model reading the first two paragraphs. Pause briefly for commas and pay particular attention to grouping words. Then have children read the next paragraph aloud.

If... children cannot read fluently without you, **then...** have them finish reading the story with you before reading it with partners.

On Their Own Pair children to do an oral reading of "The Lion and the Mouse."

Routine	Paired Reading
1. Reader 1 Begins	Reader 1 reads the story to Reader 2.
2. Reader 2 Begins	Reader 2 reads the story to Reader 1.
3. Reread	For optimal fluency, children should reread three to four times.
4. Provide Feedback	Listen to children read and provide corrective feedback. Point out any words children skip over or read incorrectly.

Provide additional practice by having children read "Checkers" on Worktext p. 71 with a partner.

Mini-Lesson 3

Fluency Goal: 65–80 words correct per minute

Remind children that...

- they should read every word accurately and at a good pace.
- quotation marks signal that characters are speaking.
- they should group words into phrases that make sense.

Guide Practice

Focus on "Hen's New Clothes" on Worktext p. 72. There are quotation marks around some groups of words. These are words that the characters are saying. Write the following words from the passage: *clothes, coins, happily, don't,* and *collecting.* Point to each word as you read it aloud. Have children follow along as you model reading the first paragraph. Before asking children to read the next paragraph with you, have them take a few moments to read the paragraph silently.

If... children cannot read fluently without you, **then...** have them finish reading the story with you before reading it with partners.

On Their Own Pair children to do an oral reading of "Hen's New Clothes."

Routine	Paired Reading
1. Reader 1 Begins	Reader 1 reads the story to Reader 2.
2. Reader 2 Begins	Reader 2 reads the story to Reader 1.
3. Reread	For optimal fluency, children should reread three to four times.
4. Provide Feedback	Listen to children read and provide corrective feedback regarding their fluency and their decoding.

For additional practice, use "Down at the Creek" on Worktext p. 73.

Expression/Intonation/Characterization 1

Objectives:
- Read with expression, or feeling, so the passage is more enjoyable to read and easier to understand.

MATERIALS

Worktext pp. 74–79
Routine Cards 2, 8
Leveled Reader Database

Set the scene

Explain expression to children. Reading with expression, or feeling, in our voices makes a passage more enjoyable to read and easier to understand. It makes the story come alive.

Model and teach

Introduce the reading passage "Fred the Frog" on Worktext p. 74. Tell children that after you have finished reading, you will ask them a question about what they read.

Explain to children that some sentences end with an exclamation mark and they should read sentences with an exclamation mark in an excited voice.
- I will read the first two sentences aloud with feeling in my voice. When I read a character's words, I will make my voice sound how I think the character would talk. I will also pause when I see a comma.
- Tell children that before you read aloud, you will first read the sentences to yourself. This helps readers become familiar with the words. Pause to read to yourself.

Have children follow along as you model reading the first two sentences expressively.

Check Comprehension

What does Fred like to do? (swim)

Remind children that...
- they should read with feeling in their voices.
- they should read every word in the passage correctly and read at a normal pace.
- sometimes a sentence continues onto the next line.

Guide Practice

Before having children read the next two sentences of "Fred the Frog" on Worktext p. 74 aloud with you, give them a few moments to read the sentences silently. Continue in this way for the remaining sentences. Remind students to sound excited when they read a sentence that ends with an exclamation point.

If... children cannot read a word,
then... have them blend decodable words **(Routine Card 2)** or say and spell high-frequency words **(Routine Card 8).**

On Their Own Prepare the group for a choral reading of "Fred the Frog." You are going to read the story aloud as a group. As you read, make sure that you read with feeling.

Routine	Choral Reading
1. Read Together	Have children read aloud with you.
2. Reread	Then have children read aloud without you. For optimal fluency, children should reread three or four times.
3. Provide Feedback	Listen to children and provide corrective feedback.

For additional practice, assign "The Library" on Worktext p. 75.

Mini-Lesson 2

Fluency Goal: 20–35 words correct per minute
Remind children that...
- they should use their voice to show feeling as they read.
- they should read every word accurately at the same speed at which they normally talk.
- sentences may continue onto the next line.

Guide Practice
Have children follow along silently as you model reading the first paragraph of "Whales" on Worktext p. 76. First, read the selected text in a monotone way. Then read it expressively. Ask children to tell which one was more interesting and discuss why. Before having children read the next paragraph aloud, give them a few moments to read the paragraph silently. Remind children to use exclamation points to guide the emotion in their voices.

If... children are unaware of their inexpressive reading,

then... model each sentence and have children repeat until they match your expression.

On Their Own Pair children to do an oral reading of "Whales."

Routine	Paired Reading
1. Reader 1 Begins	Reader 1 reads the story to Reader 2.
2. Reader 2 Begins	Reader 2 reads the story to Reader 1.
3. Reread	For optimal fluency, children should reread three to four times.
4. Provide Feedback	Listen to children read and provide corrective feedback. Point out any words children skip over or read incorrectly.

For additional practice, assign "Cats" on Worktext p. 77.

Mini-Lesson 3

Fluency Goal: 35–50 words correct per minute
Remind children that...
- they should show feeling with their voices when they read.
- they should read every word accurately and at a good pace.
- when they see an exclamation mark, they should use their voices to show excitement.

Guide Practice
Point out commas in the passage "Fun at Pine Lake" on Worktext p. 78. Commas are used to separate things in a list, such as names of people. When you come to a comma, you should pause for just a moment. Have children follow along silently as you model reading the first paragraph. Then have children read the next paragraph with you.

If... children have difficulty reading with expression,

then... ask them to tell you what happens in the story that is interesting, model an expressive reading of the paragraph containing the interesting event, and have children echo read until they match your reading.

On Their Own Pair children to do an oral reading of "Fun at Pine Lake."

Routine	Paired Reading
1. Reader 1 Begins	Reader 1 reads the story to Reader 2.
2. Reader 2 Begins	Reader 2 reads the story to Reader 1.
3. Reread	For optimal fluency, children should reread three to four times.
4. Provide Feedback	Listen to children read and provide corrective feedback regarding their fluency and their decoding.

For additional practice, use "Thanksgiving" on Worktext p. 79.

Fluency Lesson 14
Expression/Intonation/Characterization 2

Objectives:
- Read with intonation, or making your voice go up and down like natural speech.

MATERIALS
Worktext pp. 80–85
Routine Cards 2, 8
Leveled Reader Database

Set the scene Review expression with children and focus on intonation. We have practiced many skills while reading stories. Today we're going to practice reading with proper intonation. This means making our voices go up and down, just the way we do when we are talking. When we talk, our voices don't stay at one level and sound flat. We increase the loudness of our voices to show that words are very important or to show strong feeling.

Model and teach Introduce the reading passage "Tom's Best Day" on Worktext p. 80. Tell children that after you have finished reading, you will ask them a question about the passage. Point out the exclamation mark at the end of some sentences in the story. Tell children that when they read a sentence ending in an exclamation mark, their voice should show surprise or excitement.

- Tell children that you will read the first two sentences aloud. I want to make my voice go up and down to show feeling. When I read a sentence ending with an exclamation mark, my voice will sound excited or surprised.
- Tell children that before you read aloud, you will read the sentences silently. This helps readers become familiar with the words. Pause to read to yourself. Have children follow along as you model reading the first two sentences using intonation.

Check Comprehension What do Tom and his new friend do in the park? (They fly his red kite.)

Mini-Lesson 1

Fluency Goal: 50–65 words correct per minute
Remind children that...
- an exclamation mark means that they should show excitement or surprise.
- they should read with intonation, making their voices go up and down.
- they should read every word in the passage correctly and at a normal pace.

Guide Practice
Write the following words from "Tom's Best Day" on Worktext p. 80: *friend, country,* and *front.* Point to each word as you read it aloud and have children repeat after you. Then have children read the next two sentences with you. Encourage students to read with feeling and make their voices rise and fall as they read.

If... children cannot read a word,
then... have them blend decodable words (**Routine Card 2**) or say and spell high-frequency words (**Routine Card 8**).

On Their Own Prepare the group for a choral reading of "Tom's Best Day." Read with intonation, making your voice go up and down like you are talking.

Routine	Choral Reading
1. Read Together	Have children read aloud with you.
2. Reread	Then have children read aloud without you. For optimal fluency, children should reread three or four times.
3. Provide Feedback	Listen to children and provide corrective feedback.

Then assign "Fighting Fires!" on Worktext p. 81.

Mini-Lesson 2

Fluency Goal: 65–80 words correct per minute

Remind children that...

• they should use intonation to make their voices go up and down.

• they should read every word accurately at the same speed that they normally talk.

• quotation marks mean that a character is speaking.

Guide Practice

Write the following words from "The Farmer and the King" on Worktext p. 82: *bored, forgot,* and *shared.* Point to each word as you read it aloud. Have children follow along silently as you model reading the first two paragraphs. Then have children read the next paragraph aloud with you.

If... children are having difficulty using proper intonation, **then...** ask them to follow along as you read. Ask them to notice how you use your normal speaking voice but change the tone and volume. Have them echo your reading two or three times.

On Their Own Pair children to do an oral reading of "The Farmer and the King."

Routine	Paired Reading
1. Reader 1 Begins	Reader 1 reads the story to Reader 2.
2. Reader 2 Begins	Reader 2 reads the story to Reader 1.
3. Reread	For optimal fluency, children should reread three to four times.
4. Provide Feedback	Listen to children read and provide corrective feedback. Point out any words children skip over or read incorrectly.

Have children read "Help Our Earth!" on Worktext p. 83.

Mini-Lesson 3

Fluency Goal: 80–95 words correct per minute

Remind children that...

• when they see a question mark, they should make their voices go up.

• when they read, they should make voices go up and down.

• they should read accurately and at a good pace.

Guide Practice

Write the following words from "Bridges Long Ago and Today" on Worktext p. 84: *crossed, hundreds,* and *built.* Point to each word as you read it aloud. Have children follow along silently as you model reading the first paragraph. Before having children read the next paragraph with you, have them read the paragraph silently.

If... children have difficulty reading with intonation, **then...** model by asking, "Why are old bridges important to us"? Ask children which words sounded a bit louder than others. (*Why, important, us*) Model and have children echo three or four times.

On Their Own Pair children to do an oral reading of "Bridges Long Ago and Today."

Routine	Paired Reading
1. Reader 1 Begins	Reader 1 reads the story to Reader 2.
2. Reader 2 Begins	Reader 2 reads the story to Reader 1.
3. Reread	For optimal fluency, children should reread three to four times.
4. Provide Feedback	Listen to children read and provide corrective feedback regarding their fluency and their decoding.

For additional practice, use "The Girl Who Hated Noise" on Worktext p. 85.

Fluency Lesson 15
Expression/Intonation/Characterization 3

Objectives:
- Read a character's words as you think he or she would say them.

MATERIALS
Worktext pp. 86–91
Routine Cards 2, 8
Leveled Reader Database

Set the scene Review expression with children. Explain to children that as they practice reading today, they will read words that characters say in a way they think the characters would have said them. When they do this with their voices, it is called *characterization*. As they read, they will look for words that tell them about the characters. Then they will have ideas about how the characters' voices might sound and what the characters might be feeling.

Model and teach Introduce the reading passage "Hide and Seek" on Worktext p. 86. After you have finished reading, I will ask you a question about what you read.
Notice that there is an exclamation mark at the end of some sentences in the story. When you read a sentence ending in an exclamation mark, your voice should show surprise or excitement.
- Tell children you will read the first three sentences aloud. Explain that quotation marks signal the words a character says. You will look for clues about each character so you can read the words the way each character would say them.
- Before I read aloud, I will read the sentences to myself. This helps me become familiar with the words. Pause to read to yourself.
Have children follow along as you model reading the first three sentences. Give a distinct voice to each character.

Check Comprehension Who will play with James? (Will)

Mini-Lesson 1

Remind children that...
- an exclamation mark means that they should read with excitement or surprise.
- they should read each character's words as they think the character would say them.
- they should read every word in the passage correctly and read at a normal pace.

Guide Practice
Write the following words from "Hide and Seek" on Worktext p. 86: *seek, book,* and *kickball.* Point to each word as you read it aloud and have children read the words with and then read them without you. Have children read the next two sentences aloud with you.

If... children cannot read a word,
then... have them blend decodable words **(Routine Card 2)** or say and spell high-frequency words **(Routine Card 8)**.

On Their Own Prepare the group for a choral reading of "Hide and Seek." As you read, make sure that you read each character's words in the way that you think that character would say them.

Routine	Choral Reading
1. Read Together	Have children read aloud with you.
2. Reread	Then have children read aloud without you. For optimal fluency, children should reread three or four times.
3. Provide Feedback	Listen to children and provide corrective feedback.

Provide additional practice by assigning "Going to the Park" on Worktext p. 87.

Mini-Lesson 2

Fluency Goal: 20–35 words correct per minute
Remind children that...
- they should read each character's words as they think the character would say them.
- quotation marks mean that a character is speaking.
- they should read every word accurately at the same speed that they normally talk.

Guide Practice
Write the following words from "The Baseball Game" on Worktext p. 88: *baseball, ramp,* and *peanuts*. Point to each word as you read it aloud. Have children follow along silently as you model reading the first two paragraphs. Pay special attention to reading with characterization. Then have children read the next paragraph aloud with you.

If... children are having difficulty with characterization, **then...** read the second paragraph in a monotone, discuss how they might read words in a friendly way, and read the paragraph again with expression. Then have children repeat after you.

On Their Own Pair children to do an oral reading of "The Baseball Game."

Routine	Paired Reading
1. Reader 1 Begins	Reader 1 reads the story to Reader 2.
2. Reader 2 Begins	Reader 2 reads the story to Reader 1.
3. Reread	For optimal fluency, children should reread three to four times.
4. Provide Feedback	Listen to children read and provide corrective feedback. Point out any words children skip over or read incorrectly.

Assign "Wrapping a Present" on Worktext p. 89.

Mini-Lesson 3

Fluency Goal: 35–50 words correct per minute
Remind children that...
- they should read dialogue in the way they think the character would say it.
- they should read accurately and at a good pace.
- when they see a question mark, they should make their voices go up.

Guide Practice
Have children follow along silently as you model reading the first paragraph of "School Dance" on Worktext p. 90. Use different voices for Duke and June. Ask children to point out the quotation marks in the last paragraph. Then read the words between them expressively. Explain that the words outside of the quotation marks are not dialogue. Those words tell who is speaking and how they are speaking. Then have children read the next paragraph with you.

If... children have difficulty recognizing dialogue, **then...** review quotation marks as clues.

On Their Own Pair children to do an oral reading of "School Dance."

Routine	Paired Reading
1. Reader 1 Begins	Reader 1 reads the story to Reader 2.
2. Reader 2 Begins	Reader 2 reads the story to Reader 1.
3. Reread	For optimal fluency, children should reread three to four times.
4. Provide Feedback	Listen to children read and provide corrective feedback regarding their fluency and their decoding.

For additional practice, use "Show and Tell" on Worktext p. 91.

Fluency Lesson 16
Expression/Intonation/Characterization 4

Objectives:
- Read with expression, making your voice louder and quieter, stressing important words, and using a distinct voice for each character.

MATERIALS

Worktext pp. 92–97
Routine Cards 2, 8
Leveled Reader Database

Set the scene Review expression with children. You've been practicing skills to make you better readers. Today we will read with expression and use our voices to make the story interesting. We'll practice correct intonation by changing our voices in tone and loudness, just like we do when we are talking. When we read different characters' words, we'll use different voices. Practicing all these skills together will make us better readers. It's fun too!

Model and teach Introduce the reading passage "Sam the Snowman" on Worktext p. 92.
Tell children that after they have finished reading, you will ask them a question about what they read.
Explain to children that in this story they will find some exclamation marks. When a sentence ends with an exclamation mark, they should show surprise or excitement in their voices.
- Tell children that you will read aloud the first three paragraphs. You will look for clues about each character because you want to read the words in quotation marks the way each character would say them.
- Before I read aloud, I will take a moment to read the sentences to myself. This helps me become familiar with the words. Pause to read to yourself.
Have children follow along as you model reading the first three paragraphs. Give a distinct voice to each character.

Check Comprehension Who tells Anna and Ben that it will be a sunny day? (their mom)

Fluency Goal: 50–65 words correct per minute
Remind children that…
- they should read each character's words as they think the character would say them.
- they should read every word in the passage correctly and read at a normal pace.
- they should vary their volume and tone to make their reading more interesting.

Guide Practice
Continue reading "Sam the Snowman" on Worktext p. 92. Before having children read the next two paragraphs aloud with you, give them a few moments to read the sentences silently. Remind them to change their voice for each character.

If… children cannot read a word,

then… have them blend decodable words (Routine Card 2) or say and spell high-frequency words (Routine Card 8).

On Their Own Prepare the group for a choral reading of "Sam the Snowman." Read with expression and read each character's words in the way that you think that character would say them.

Routine	Choral Reading
1. Read Together **2. Reread**	Have children read aloud with you. Then have children read aloud without you. For optimal fluency, children should reread three or four times.
3. Provide Feedback	Listen to children and provide corrective feedback.

Provide additional practice by assigning "At the Parade" on Worktext p. 93.

Mini-Lesson 2

Fluency Goal: 65–80 words correct per minute
Remind children that...

• they should read each character's words like they think the character would say them.
• they should show expression with their voices and vary volume and tone to make the story interesting.
• they should read every word accurately at the same speed that they normally talk.

Guide Practice

Write the following words from "What Can You See at the Park?" on Worktext p. 94: *Mrs., excited, Darnel,* and *maple.* Point to each word as you read it aloud and have children repeat after you. Next, read the selected text stiffly and then model correct characterization. Point out that reading with characterization makes a story easier to understand. Then have children read the first paragraph aloud with you.

If... children are reading stiffly or in a monotone, **then...** ask them to read as if they are talking, model reading the passage again, and have children repeat until fluent.

On Their Own Pair children to do an oral reading of "What Can You See at the Park?"

Routine	Paired Reading
1. Reader 1 Begins	Reader 1 reads the story to Reader 2.
2. Reader 2 Begins	Reader 2 reads the story to Reader 1.
3. Reread	For optimal fluency, children should reread three to four times.
4. Provide Feedback	Listen to children read and provide corrective feedback. Point out any words children skip over or read incorrectly.

Assign "At the Pond" on Worktext p. 95.

Mini-Lesson 3

Fluency Goal: 80–95 words correct per minute
Remind children that...

• they should read dialogue in the way they think the character would say it.
• they should use a lot of expression in their voices and make the story interesting.
• they should read accurately and at a good pace.

Guide Practice

Before introducing the reading passage "A Big Surprise!" on Worktext p. 96, make sure that children understand that an art show is a place where drawings and other types of art are displayed. Have children follow along silently as you model reading the first paragraph. Give a distinct voice to the character of Lavon. Point out how small changes in your voice can make each character come alive in the story. Have children read the next two paragraphs with you.

If... children have difficulty with characterization, **then...** model the text again and have children repeat three or four times.

On Their Own Pair children to do an oral reading of "A Big Surprise!"

Routine	Paired Reading
1. Reader 1 Begins	Reader 1 reads the story to Reader 2.
2. Reader 2 Begins	Reader 2 reads the story to Reader 1.
3. Reread	For optimal fluency, children should reread three to four times.
4. Provide Feedback	Listen to children read and provide corrective feedback regarding their fluency and their decoding.

For additional practice, use "The Pizza Project" on Worktext p. 97.

Fluency Lesson 17
Fluency 1

Objectives:
- Read text quickly, accurately, and with expression.

MATERIALS

Worktext pp. 98–103
Routine Cards 2, 8
Leveled Reader Database

Set the scene Review fluency with children. We have practiced different reading skills. Today we will put these skills together to practice fluent reading. Tell children they will practice reading all the words correctly and at a normal rate. They should try not to rush or read too slowly. They should sound as if they are explaining something to someone. They will also practice reading with expression, or feeling, so the passage comes alive.

Model and teach Introduce the reading passage "Class Pet" on Worktext p. 98. Tell children that after they have finished reading, you will ask them a question about what the story. Explain to children that sometimes a line ends without punctuation. This means that the sentence continues onto the next line. Children should read to the end of the line and then continue reading right away on the next line.

- Tell children that you will read the first three sentences aloud without mistakes. You will also use the same rate of speed you use when you talk. I will read with expression and put a lot of feeling into my voice.
- Before I read aloud, I will first read the sentences to myself to become familiar with the words. Pause to read to yourself.

Have children follow along silently as you model reading the first three sentences without mistakes and at a normal rate. Pay special attention to reading expressively.

Check Comprehension Who likes to pet Elsie? (Tyrone and Robin)

Mini-Lesson 1

Remind children that...
- they should read every word in the passage correctly and read at a normal pace.
- they should vary their volume and tone to make their reading more interesting.
- they should group words into phrases that make sense.

Guide Practice
Start by having children read the next two sentences of "Class Pet" on Worktext p. 98 aloud with you. Give them a few moments to read the sentences silently. Continue in this way for the remaining sentences.

If... children cannot read a word,
then... have them blend decodable words **(Routine Card 2)** or say and spell high-frequency words **(Routine Card 8)**.

On Their Own Prepare the group for a choral reading of "Class Pet." Remember to show expression and read every word accurately. Read at the same rate you would use when talking to a friend.

Routine	Choral Reading
1. Read Together	Have children read aloud with you.
2. Reread	Then have children read aloud without you. For optimal fluency, children should reread three or four times.
3. Provide Feedback	Listen to children and provide corrective feedback.

For additional practice, assign "Father's Day" on Worktext p. 99.

Mini-Lesson 2

Fluency Goal: 20–35 words correct per minute

Remind children that...

- they should read every word accurately at the same speed that they normally talk.
- they should read each character's words as they think the character would say them.
- they should show expression with their voices and vary volume and tone.

Guide Practice

Introduce the story "Kate Is Late" on Worktext p. 100. There are commas and exclamation marks in some sentences. When we come to a comma, we should pause for just a second before continuing to read. An exclamation mark tells us that the sentence should be read with surprise or excitement in our voices. Then have children read the first paragraph aloud with you.

If... children are reading very slowly,

then... ask them to read the selected text again and track the print. Then have them take away their fingers and read the text again as if they were talking to a friend. Discuss which reading sounds better. Model and have children repeat.

On Their Own Pair children to do an oral reading of "Kate Is Late."

Routine	Paired Reading
1. Reader 1 Begins	Reader 1 reads the story to Reader 2.
2. Reader 2 Begins	Reader 2 reads the story to Reader 1.
3. Reread	For optimal fluency, children should reread three to four times. Listen to children read and provide corrective feedback. Point out any words children skip over or read incorrectly.
4. Provide Feedback	

For additional practice, assign "Bedtime" on Worktext p. 101.

Mini-Lesson 3

Fluency Goal: 35–50 words correct per minute

Remind children that...

- they should read accurately and at a good pace.
- they should make their voices go up and down as if they are talking.
- they should read words in quotation marks in the way they think the character would say them.

Guide Practice

Before turning to "Five White Mice" on Worktext p. 102, review the purpose of quotation marks with children. Remind them that quotation marks show when someone is talking. Before having children read the next two paragraphs with you, give them a few moments to read the paragraphs silently.

If... children substitute a word,

then... point to the misidentified word, sound it out,

and read it correctly. Then model the entire sentence and have children repeat after you.

On Their Own Pair children to do an oral reading of "Five White Mice."

Routine	Paired Reading
1. Reader 1 Begins	Reader 1 reads the story to Reader 2.
2. Reader 2 Begins	Reader 2 reads the story to Reader 1.
3. Reread	For optimal fluency, children should reread three to four times. Listen to children read and provide corrective feedback regarding their fluency and their decoding.
4. Provide Feedback	

For additional practice, use "Rex the Pest" on Worktext p. 103.

Fluency Lesson 18
Fluency 2

Objectives:

- Read text quickly, accurately, and with expression.

MATERIALS

Worktext pp. 104–109
Routine Cards 2, 8
Leveled Reader Database

Set the scene Review fluency with children. Tell children that today they will practice reading all the words correctly while they read at the speed they use when talking. They will also practice reading with expression in their voices. By practicing these reading skills, they will become better readers.

Model and teach Introduce the reading passage "Where Will Jin Go?" on Worktext p. 104. After you have finished reading, I will ask you a question about what you read. Tell children to notice that there is a question mark at the end of some of the sentences. When they read a sentence ending in a question mark, they should make their voices go up at the end of the sentence.

- I will read the first two paragraphs aloud without making any mistakes. Words in quotation marks mean a character is speaking. I will read these words to show what I think the character is feeling.
- Before I read aloud, I will first read the sentences to myself. This helps me become familiar with the words. Pause to read to yourself.

Have children follow along silently as you model reading the first two paragraphs with no mistakes. Read in a natural tone of voice and use your voice expressively.

Check Comprehension What do the bears do at the zoo? (splash and play in the water)

Mini-Lesson 1

Fluency Goal: 50–65 words correct per minute
Remind children that...

- they should read every word in the passage correctly and quickly.
- they should show what the character is feeling.
- they should make their voices go up and down like natural speech.

Guide Practice
Write the following words from "Where Will Jin Go?" on Worktext p. 104: *surprise, tomorrow, animals,* and *horses.* Point to each word as you read it aloud and have children repeat after you. Then have children read the next three paragraphs aloud with you.

If... children cannot read a word,
then... have them blend decodable words **(Routine Card 2)** or say and spell high-frequency words **(Routine Card 8).**

On Their Own Prepare the group for a choral reading of "Where Will Jin Go." Make each character sound different. Read every word accurately and group them in ways that make sense. Read at the same rate you would use when talking to a friend.

Routine	Choral Reading
1. **Read Together**	Have children read aloud with you.
2. **Reread**	Then have children read aloud without you. For optimal fluency, children should reread three or four times.
3. **Provide Feedback**	Listen to children and provide corrective feedback.

For additional practice, assign "Miniature Golf" on Worktext p. 105.

Mini-Lesson 2

Fluency Goal: 65–80 words correct per minute

Remind children that...

- they should read every word accurately at the same speed that they normally talk.
- they should read each character's words as they think the character would say them.
- they should show expression with their voices to make the story interesting.

Guide Practice

Introduce the story "Sick Day" on Worktext p. 106. Notice that some sentences have quotation marks in them. Quotation marks show that someone is speaking. Think about what each character is thinking and try to make your voice sound like how you think the character would sound. Then have children read aloud the first two paragraphs with you.

If... children cannot read expressively without you,

then... model reading the story correctly and have children echo your reading.

On Their Own Pair children to do an oral reading of "Sick Day."

Routine	Paired Reading
1. Reader 1 Begins	Reader 1 reads the story to Reader 2.
2. Reader 2 Begins	Reader 2 reads the story to Reader 1.
3. Reread	For optimal fluency, children should reread three to four times.
4. Provide Feedback	Listen to children read and provide corrective feedback. Point out any words children skip over or read incorrectly.

For additional practice, "Ellie Takes Pictures" on Worktext p. 107.

Mini-Lesson 3

Fluency Goal: 80–95 words correct per minute

Remind children that...

- they should read accurately and not skip over any words.
- they should group words in phrases that make sense.
- they should read dialogue in the way they think the character would say it.

Guide Practice

Have children follow along as you model the first three paragraphs of "A Lamb Named Happy" on Worktext p. 108. Pay attention to accuracy, rate, expression, and phrasing. Give a distinct voice to Cady. Before having children read the next two paragraphs aloud with you, give them a few moments to read the paragraphs silently.

If... children are skipping over or substituting words,

then... ask them to track the print as you model selected text. Then have them echo your reading without tracking.

On Their Own Pair children to do an oral reading of "A Lamb Named Happy."

Routine	Paired Reading
1. Reader 1 Begins	Reader 1 reads the story to Reader 2.
2. Reader 2 Begins	Reader 2 reads the story to Reader 1.
3. Reread	For optimal fluency, children should reread three to four times.
4. Provide Feedback	Listen to children read and provide corrective feedback regarding their fluency and their decoding.

For additional practice, use "Dinosaurs" on Worktext p. 109.

Fluency Lesson 19
Fluency 3

Objectives:
- Read text quickly, accurately, and with expression.

MATERIALS

Worktext pp. 110–115
Routine Cards 2, 8
Leveled Reader Database

Set the scene

Review fluency with children. When someone reads a story to you, you like the story to sound interesting and you want to understand every word. Tell children that today they will practice reading a story with expression. To make sure they understand what is happening in the story, they will read every word correctly and not read too fast or too slow. As children practice these reading skills, they will find that it becomes easier and more fun!

Model and teach

Introduce the reading passage "Fred the Farmer" on Worktext p. 110. After you have finished reading, I will ask you a question about what you read.

Tell children that there is a period at the end of each sentence. A period means that they're at the end of the sentence, so they should stop for just a moment.

- I will read the first two sentences aloud. I want to read without making any mistakes. I will read with feeling to make the story interesting and to better understand it.
- Before I read aloud, I will read the sentences to myself. This helps me become familiar with the words. Pause to read to yourself.

Have children follow along silently as you model reading the first two sentences with no mistakes. Read in a natural tone of voice and use your voice expressively.

Check Comprehension

What animals does Fred feed? (cow, pig, and dog)

Mini-Lesson 1

Remind children that…
- they should read every word in the passage correctly and quickly.
- when they see a period at the end of a sentence, they should pause.
- they should make their voices go up and down like natural speech.

Guide Practice

Continue reading "Fred the Farmer" on Worktext p. 110. Before having children read the next two sentences aloud with you, give them a few moments to read the sentences silently.

If… children cannot read a word,
then… have them blend decodable words **(Routine Card 2)** or say and spell high-frequency words **(Routine Card 8)**.

On Their Own Prepare the group for a choral reading of "Fred the Farmer." Make your voice go up and down to show feeling. Read every word accurately and group them in ways that make sense. Read at the same rate you would use when talking to a friend.

Routine	Choral Reading
1. Read Together	Have children read aloud with you.
2. Reread	Then have children read aloud without you. For optimal fluency, children should reread three or four times.
3. Provide Feedback	Listen to children and provide corrective feedback.

Provide additional practice by assigning "The Big Race" on Worktext p. 111.

Mini-Lesson 2

Fluency Goal: 20–35 words correct per minute

Remind children that...

- they should read every word accurately at the same speed that they normally talk.
- they should show expression with their voices to make the story interesting.
- they should read silently to themselves first to become familiar with the words.

Guide Practice

Review periods, exclamation marks, and question marks with children. Remember to pause when you see a period at the end of a sentence. Make your voice go up when a sentence ends with a question mark. Show excitement or surprise when you see an exclamation mark. Before having children read aloud the first paragraph of "Gus Runs" on Worktext p. 112, have them read the paragraph silently.

If... children skip a word,

then... point to the word, sound it out, read it correctly, model the entire sentence, and have children repeat it after you.

On Their Own Pair children to do an oral reading of "Gus Runs."

Routine	Paired Reading
1. Reader 1 Begins	Reader 1 reads the story to Reader 2.
2. Reader 2 Begins	Reader 2 reads the story to Reader 1.
3. Reread	For optimal fluency, children should reread three to four times. Listen to children read and provide corrective feedback. Point out any words children skip over or read incorrectly.
4. Provide Feedback	

For additional practice, assign "A Surprise for Charlie" on Worktext p. 113.

Mini-Lesson 3

Fluency Goal: 35–50 words correct per minute

Remind children that...

- they should read accurately and not skip over any words.
- they should group words in phrases that make sense.
- they should read with feeling to make the story more interesting.

Guide Practice

Have children follow along as you model reading the first two paragraphs of "Dog Show" on Worktext p. 114. Pay attention to accuracy, rate, expression, and phrasing. Before having children read the next two paragraphs aloud with you, give them a few moments to read the paragraphs silently.

If... children have difficulty using their voices expressively,

then... read the second paragraph in a monotone. Then read it expressively. Ask which was more interesting and easier to understand. Model the paragraph again and have children repeat it after you.

On Their Own Pair children to do an oral reading of "Dog Show."

Routine	Paired Reading
1. Reader 1 Begins	Reader 1 reads the story to Reader 2.
2. Reader 2 Begins	Reader 2 reads the story to Reader 1.
3. Reread	For optimal fluency, children should reread three to four times. Listen to children read and provide corrective feedback regarding their fluency and their decoding.
4. Provide Feedback	

For additional practice, use "Horses" on Worktext p. 115.

Fluency Lesson 20
Fluency 4

Objectives:
- Read text quickly, accurately, and with expression.

MATERIALS
Worktext pp. 116–121
Routine Card 2
Leveled Reader Database

Set the scene
Review fluency with children. Tell children they will practice reading all the words correctly and at a speed that sounds like when they're talking. They'll practice intonation, or the way their voices rise and fall naturally as they speak or read. They will also read story characters' words to show how they think the characters are feeling.

Model and teach
Introduce the reading passage "The Country Mouse and the City Mouse" on Worktext p. 116. After you have finished reading, I will ask you a question about what you read.

Tell children that there are quotation marks around some groups of words. These are words that the story characters are saying.

- I will read the first paragraph aloud without making any mistakes and at a natural speed. I will let the volume of my voice rise and fall naturally. I will read a character's words with expression.
- Before I read aloud, I will take a moment to read the paragraph to myself. This helps me become familiar with the words. Pause to read to yourself.

Have children follow along silently as you model reading the first paragraph with no mistakes. Pay special attention to intonation and reading the character's words expressively.

Check Comprehension
What happens after the mice begin to eat? (A cat races into the room.)

Mini-Lesson 1

Fluency Goal: 50–65 words correct per minute
Remind children that...
- they should read every word in the passage correctly and at a natural speed.
- they should remember that quotation marks around groups of words show that a character is speaking.
- they should make their voices go up and down as if they are talking to someone.

Guide Practice
Continue reading "The Country Mouse and the City Mouse" on Worktext p. 116. Before having children read aloud the next paragraph with you, have them read the sentences silently. Continue in this way for the remaining paragraphs.

If... children cannot read a word,
then... have them blend decodable words
(Routine Card 2).

On Their Own Prepare the group for a choral reading of "The Country Mouse and the City Mouse." Make sure that you change the volume of your voice as you read, like you do when you talk. Read what the story characters say with expression.

Routine	Choral Reading
1. Read Together	Have children read aloud with you.
2. Reread	Then have children read aloud without you. For optimal fluency, children should reread three or four times.
3. Provide Feedback	Listen to children and provide corrective feedback.

Provide additional practice by assigning "Loose Tooth" on Worktext p. 117.

Mini-Lesson 2

Fluency Goal: 65–80 words correct per minute
Remind children that...
- they should read every word accurately at the same speed that they normally talk.
- when they see an exclamation mark, they should read with excitement or surprise.
- they should first read silently to themselves to become familiar with the words.

Guide Practice
Focus on "Patrick Goes to the Movies" on Worktext p. 118. Review periods and exclamation marks with children. Remember to read with excitement or surprise when you see an exclamation mark. Before having children read aloud the first paragraph, have them read the paragraph silently. Continue in this way for the remaining paragraphs.

If... children have difficulty reading with appropriate intonation,

then... model selected sentences and have them echo read three or four times. Point out that with practice, their intonation will improve.

On Their Own Pair children to do an oral reading of "Patrick Goes to the Movies."

Routine	Paired Reading
1. Reader 1 Begins	Reader 1 reads the story to Reader 2.
2. Reader 2 Begins	Reader 2 reads the story to Reader 1.
3. Reread	For optimal fluency, children should reread three to four times.
4. Provide Feedback	Listen to children read and provide corrective feedback. Point out any words children skip over or read incorrectly.

For additional practice, "Lost in the Forest" on Worktext p. 119.

Mini-Lesson 3

Fluency Goal: 80–95 words correct per minute
Remind children that...
- they should every word accurately and at a natural pace.
- they should group words in phrases that make sense.
- they should read with expression to make the story more interesting.

Guide Practice
Make sure that children know that an astronomer studies space and a telescope is an instrument that allows scientists to look far out into space. Have children follow along as you model reading the first paragraph of "Pluto" on Worktext p. 120. Pay attention to accuracy, rate, expression, and phrasing. Before having children read the next paragraph aloud with you, give them a few moments to read the paragraphs silently.

If... children cannot read fluently without you,

then... have them track the print as they finish reading the story with you before reading it with a partner.

On Their Own Pair children to do an oral reading of "Pluto."

Routine	Paired Reading
1. Reader 1 Begins	Reader 1 reads the story to Reader 2.
2. Reader 2 Begins	Reader 2 reads the story to Reader 1.
3. Reread	For optimal fluency, children should reread three to four times.
4. Provide Feedback	Listen to children read and provide corrective feedback regarding their fluency and their decoding.

For additional practice, use "The Grand Canyon" on Worktext p. 121.

Fluency Student Worktext

At Bat

Pig is at bat.   4
Can Pig get a hit?   9

Pig got a hit.   13
Pig ran and ran.   17

Dog is at bat.   21
Can Dog get a hit?   26

Dog got a hit.   30
Dog ran and ran.   34

Cat got a hit.   38
Will Pig, Dog, and Cat win?   44

Directions Read the story "At Bat" to your child. Then have your child practice reading the story with you until he or she can read it without mistakes. Make sure your child pauses briefly for periods and question marks.

Pets on Jets

Kate has a pet cat.	5
Kate calls him Red.	9
Mother and Kate get on a big jet.	17
Can Red get on the jet?	23
Cats cannot get on big jets.	29
Kate is sad.	32
Can a man help Red?	37
The man will help Red.	42
Can Red get in a pet box?	49
The pet box can go on the jet.	57

School + Home **Directions** Read the story "Pets on Jets" to your child. Then have your child practice reading the story with you until he or she can read it without mistakes.

Name _____

Six Big Frogs

Six big frogs hop on one	6
big stick.	8
Six big frogs spot six	13
big bees.	15
Six big bees fly around	20
the big stick.	23
They fly away	26
when they see the frogs.	31
Six big frogs hop	35
as fast as they may.	40
They try to catch	44
the bees that flew away.	49
Six big frogs open	53
their mouths. They snap!	57
The six big bees	61
never had a chance.	65

Directions Read the story "Six Big Frogs" to your child. Pay particular attention to reading each word clearly. Then ask your child to read it back to you without making any mistakes.

Jen the Vet

Jen the vet likes hens.   5

She feeds a hen named Ben.   11

Jen pets Ben the hen.   16

Jen the vet likes pigs too.   22

She met Blue the pig at a zoo.   30

Jen pets and feeds Blue too.   36

Jack is my pet cat.   41

Jen always gives Jack a snap.   47

She likes to pet Jack on his back.   55

Jen the vet feeds Ben, Blue, and Jack.   63

She pets their heads and backs.   69

Ben, Blue, and Jack love Jen the vet.   77

School + Home

Directions Take turns reading the story "Jen the Vet" aloud with your child. Read the story at least two or three times. Remind your child to read every word and read it correctly. Make sure your child pauses for a moment for periods.

Luke and Jack See Granddad

Dad, Luke, and Jack ride in a jeep. They are on a trip to   14
see Granddad.   16

"See that?" asks Dad.   20

"Yes, I can see six sheep!" calls Luke.   28

"See that?" asks Dad.   32

"Yes, I can see two trucks," Jack tells him.   41

"See that bobcat?" Jack asks Luke. "It is in back of that   53
tree." The bobcat jumps out and runs by the jeep.   63

"I wish Granddad could see that!" Luke yells. "Can we   73
bring him here?"   76

"See that?" asks Dad. Luke sees Granddad.   83

"Granddad!" yell Luke and Jack. "Do you want to see a   94
bobcat? Let's go!"   97

Directions Read the story "Luke and Jack See Granddad" to your child, using a different voice for each character. Then ask your child to read the story to you without making any mistakes.

Helping Hope Shop

Dad, Mom, and Hope went to shop. Dad drove the car.   11
Hope rode in the back.   16

"Is the shop close?" asked Hope.   22

"Yes, it is, Hope," said Mom.   28

They went into the shop. Hope went to a big shelf.   39
She saw toy bears, horses, and pigs. Then she saw a   50
big rabbit!   52

"I have a small toy rabbit at home," said Hope. "Can I get   65
the big rabbit?"   68

Hope saw Dad and Mom smile. Mom said, "You can get   79
the big rabbit. You chose well."   85

Hope held the rabbit close. "This rabbit will fit in at   96
home. Thanks, Mom! Thanks, Dad!"   101

Directions Take turns reading the story "Helping Hope Shop" aloud with your child. Then have your child practice reading it without making any mistakes. Make sure your child pauses for a moment for periods, question marks, and exclamation points.

School + Home

The Fox and the Crow

One day Crow sat in a tall tree with a big piece of bread in her   16
mouth. Fox soon had a plan to get the bread from Crow.   28

"Hello, friend!" Fox called to Crow.   34

But Crow could not say a word. The bread filled her mouth.   46

"You are very beautiful," said Fox. "You could be the   56
queen of the birds!"   60

The crow nodded her head.   65

"But a queen needs a big voice. Too bad you do not have   78
one," Fox said.   81

Crow opened her mouth wide to speak. When she did,   91
the bread fell to the ground. Then Fox took it. He ran away.   104

Do not be tricked by sweet words!   111

School + Home **Directions** Read the fable to your child. Then ask your child to read it without making any mistakes.

School Bus

I ride the school bus every day. I like the school bus. 12
It is yellow. It has many seats. 19

The driver is Mrs. Hill. She smiles at me. "Good morning," 30
she says. 32

"Good morning," I say. Then I sit down. I sit with Mike. 44
He is my best friend. We go to the same school. Mike is 57
also on my soccer team. 62

We talk all the way to school. When the bus stops, 73
we get out. Mrs. Hill counts us. 80

We line up in front of our teacher. Mrs. Johnson is nice. 92
She smiles too. She leads us inside. 99

The bell rings. It is time to learn. 107

School + Home

Directions Take turns reading the story "School Bus" aloud with your child. Read the story at least two or three times. Remind your child to read every word and read it correctly. Make sure your child pauses for a moment for periods.

The Loose Tooth

Juan had a loose tooth. He wiggled it with his tongue.	11
He wiggled it with his finger. He wiggled it at school.	22
He wiggled it at home. He wiggled it on the bus.	33

Juan wanted the tooth to fall out. Then he could give it to	46
the Tooth Fairy. If he put his tooth under his pillow, she	58
would take it. She would give him money.	66

Juan wiggled the tooth all week. One day he was riding	77
the bus. Pop! The tooth fell out. Juan was happy. Soon	88
he would have a new tooth.	94

Juan showed the tooth to his mother. "Put it under	104
your pillow," she said.	108

He showed it to his sister. "Oh!" she said.	117

Juan showed it to his father. "Put it under your pillow,"	128
he said.	130

So Juan put it under his pillow. He was excited. He was	142
tired too. Soon Juan fell asleep. In the morning, the tooth	153
was gone. There was a dollar!	159

Directions Read the story "The Loose Tooth" to your child, using a different voice for each character. Then ask your child to read the story to you without making any mistakes.

Name _____

Ant Farm

Our class got a big surprise last week. Our teacher brought   11
an ant farm into our room. An ant farm is not a real farm.   25
It is a big glass box full of blue gel.   35

Our teacher put 20 ants inside the box. The ants walked   46
around the top. They started digging, and they made   55
tunnels in the gel. They ate the gel too.   64

Every day we watch the ants. We measure their tunnels   74
with a ruler. Our teacher takes pictures of the tunnels.   84

We read a book about ants. There are many kinds of ants.   96
Ants can be red or black. Our ants are black. Ants have   108
six legs. Ants have a hard shell. They have no ears.   119
Some ants have wings.   123

Ants are strong. They can carry very heavy things. Ants   133
can work together. They live in groups, and the groups   143
have a queen. She is their mother.   150

Watch out! Ants can bite! Some ants eat plants. Other ants   161
eat animals. Ants have to look for food.   169

Directions Read the story "Ant Farm" to your child. Then have your child practice reading the story with you until he or she can read it without mistakes.

Fluency Lesson 2   Accuracy 2 **11**

Leah's Farm

Leah lives on a farm. She grows corn, beans, and hay on her   13
farm. She has a big vegetable garden.   20

There are animals living on the farm too. Two horses,   30
four goats, six dogs, eight cats, and ten chickens live on   41
the farm. Leah takes good care of the animals.   50

Every morning, Leah feeds the animals. She feeds hay to the   61
horses and corn to the goats. She feeds dog food to the dogs   74
and cat food to the cats. She drops corn on the ground for   87
the chickens.   89

All day long, Leah works on the farm. She plants seeds.   100
Leah harvests crops. She cleans the barn. She grooms   109
the horses. Leah milks the goats. She gathers eggs from the   120
chickens. Leah mends the fences. Then she mows the grass.   130

All day long, the animals play on the farm. The horses chase   142
the goats. The goats chase the dogs. The dogs chase the   153
cats. The cats chase the chickens. The chickens chase   162
the flies that buzz around the barn.   169

At the end of the day, everyone is very tired. Leah puts the   182
sleepy animals in the barn and says goodnight.   190

Directions Read the story "Leah's Farm" to your child. Encourage your child to practice reading until he or she can read the entire story without making mistakes. Make sure your child reads in a way that sounds like natural speech.

Name _____

Nick's Trains

Nick likes model trains. He has 15 model train cars   10
and 3 engines. Nick is proud of his trains. His grandpa   21
bought Nick his first train on his fourth birthday. Nick loves   32
to go to the model train shop with his grandpa. They like   44
to watch the trains run. Sometimes they buy a new car   55
for Nick's trains.   58

Once a month, Nick brings his trains to the library. Nick's   69
grandpa is part of a train club. The club members all bring   81
their trains too. They set up all the trains on tracks in the   94
library. They put tiny people, trees, and bridges along the   104
tracks.   105

Kids come with their parents to watch the trains. Nick likes   116
to tell other kids about the trains. Each one is special.   127
Nick's favorite is his steam engine. It puffs steam as it   138
rolls down the tracks. Nick likes spending time with his   148
grandpa and his trains.   152

Nick's little brother Jake likes trains too. Nick reads   161
books about trains to Jake. Someday Jake will have his   171
own trains.   173

School + Home

Directions Take turns reading the story "Nick's Trains" aloud with your child. Then have your child practice reading it without making any mistakes. Make sure your child pauses for a moment for periods, question marks, and exclamation points.

Little Sister

I have a little sister.   5
What is her name?   9
Her name is Eva.   13

Eva is pretty.   16
She is a baby.   20
Her eyes are blue.   24

Can Eva play with toys?   29
She plays with a ball.   34
She plays with a bear.   39
I like to play with Eva.   45

School + Home **Directions** Read the story "Little Sister" to your child. Read the story as if you are talking to your child. Then have your child practice reading the story with you.

Paul and the Red Ball

Paul has a red ball.	5
Paul throws the ball.	9
The ball hits a wall.	14
Sam sees the ball.	18
Sam throws the red ball down the hall.	26
Paul runs down the hall.	31
Where is the ball?	35
Paul cannot see the ball.	40
Paul is sad.	43
Sam looks for the ball.	48
Sam finds the ball.	52
Paul and Sam are happy.	57

School + Home

Directions Read the story "Paul and the Red Ball" to your child. Then have your child practice reading the story with you until he or she can read it at the same speed he or she uses when talking.

Duck Pond

The sun is hot.	4
It is hot at Duck Pond.	10
Ducks land on Duck Pond	15
with a big splash!	19
Ducks like to swim.	23
Ducks jump in Duck Pond	28
and get wet.	31
Ducks go *splat!*	34
Ducks get small fish to eat	40
in Duck Pond.	43
Ducks snack on bugs!	47
Ducks rest at Duck Pond.	52
Ducks pick snug resting spots	57
and nap.	59
It is fun at Duck Pond.	65

Directions Read the story "Duck Pond" to your child at the same speed you use when talking. Then have your child practice reading it at the same speed he or she uses when talking.

Fluency Lesson 3

Name _____

Petting Zoo

Evan and Sofie go   4
to the petting zoo.   8
Sofie pets a rabbit   12
and Evan pets a sheep.   17

Sofie feeds the rabbit   21
and pets its head.   25
The rabbit has gray fur   30
and a white tail.   34

Evan feeds the sheep.   38
The sheep is soft.   42
The sheep is white   46
and says, "Baa."   49

Sofie sees a brown duck.   54
The duck has orange feet.   59

Evan and Sofie love the petting zoo.   66

Directions Take turns reading the story "Petting Zoo" aloud with your child. Read the story at least two or three times. Remind your child to read at the same rate that he or she normally speaks. Make sure your child pauses for a moment for periods.

Dean's Neat Green Cast

Dean and Sid like to race on sleds. When they race, Dean   12
likes to beat Sid.   16

One time, Dean went very fast. "Look how fast I am going!"   28
called Dean. Then Dean's sled tipped. Dean's leg was hurt.   38

Dad took Dean to see Doc Jean. She looked at his leg.   50

"Bones are like a frame. They don't bend," Doc Jean said.   61
"You broke your leg. I will put on a cast. That will help it heal."   76

Doc Jean asked Dean to pick his cast. He chose a green   88
cast. "Green is neat," he said.   94

Dean had the cast for six weeks. There were no more   105
sled rides that winter!   109

Directions Read the story "Dean's Neat Green Cast" to your child at your normal rate of speaking. Pay particular attention to using your voice expressively when reading dialogue. Then ask your child to read the story to you without making any mistakes and at a normal rate.

Name _____   Rate 1 _____

Emma Learns to Skate

Emma wanted to learn how to skate. She asked her mom   11
for skates. "Maybe you will get them for your birthday,"   21
her mom said.   24

Emma got purple skates and a helmet for her birthday.   34
She was very excited.   38

"Will you teach me to skate?" Emma asked her mom.   48
"Yes," her mom said.   52

Emma went outside. She put on her skates and helmet.   62
Emma started skating down the sidewalk. She went too   71
fast and fell down. Ouch!   76

Emma's mom held her hand. She helped Emma skate   85
slower. Then she taught Emma how to stop.   93

Emma skated every day. Her mom helped. Soon   101
she didn't need help. Emma had learned how to skate.   111

Directions Take turns reading the story "Emma Learns to Skate" aloud with your child. Then have your child practice reading it quickly. Make sure your child pauses for a moment for periods, question marks, and exclamation points.

Fluency Lesson 3   Rate 1 **19**

A New Garden

Dad, Taye, and Nita helped plant a new garden in the park.	12
Their dog Cody watched them work.	18
"Do not get in our way," Dad said to Cody. Cody barked and	31
wagged his tail. He watched Taye and Nita dig.	40
They planted different kinds of seeds. "These seeds will	49
grow into beautiful flowers," Taye said to Cody. Cody barked	59
and wagged his tail.	63
"These seeds will grow into tall, green grass," Nita said to	74
Cody. Cody barked again and wagged his tail. Then he	84
jumped into an empty part of the garden. He started to dig.	96
Soon dirt filled the air.	101
"Look at Cody! He's helping us. Now we can plant more	112
seeds!" Dad said.	115

School + Home **Directions** Read the story to your child. Then ask your child to read it to you as if he or she were speaking to someone.

Car Wash

"You have chores to do," Joe's mother said.   8

"What chores?" Joe asked.   12

"You can wash the car. Ask your dad for help," she said.   24

Joe found his dad in the kitchen. "Will you help me wash   36
the car?" he asked.   40

"Yes. Let's go," Joe's dad said.   46

Joe and his dad went outside. Joe's dad got a bucket and   58
soap. Joe got towels and rags.   64

Joe's dad filled the bucket with soap and water. They used   75
the wet rags to wash the car. Joe washed the wheels.   86
His dad washed the windows. They both washed the doors.   96
Joe and his dad dried the car with dry towels.   106

The car was clean. Joe had fun and his mother was happy.   118

School + Home **Directions** Read the story "Car Wash" to your child. Then have your child practice reading the story with you until he or she can read it at a normal pace.

At the Circus

Today Mother will take Alonso and his best friend Carlos to   11
the circus.   13

"I want to see the elephants, and Carlos wants to see the   25
clowns," Alonso says.   28

First, the children watch the clowns in the big tent. It is fun   41
to see six clowns riding one small, red bike.   50

A smiling clown stops in front of Alonso and Carlos. He   61
throws four bright orange balls high in the air. Carlos catches   72
one ball, and Alonso catches another one. The children both   82
throw balls back to the clown.   88

Then Alonso, Carlos, and Mother see the elephants.   96
The big animals walk proudly around the tent. Everyone   105
claps and cheers!   108

"Look at the elephants stand on their back legs!" says Carlos.   119

At the end of the day, Carlos and Alonso are tired but   131
happy. Tomorrow they will tell their friends about their visit   141
to the circus.   144

Directions Read the story in your normal speaking voice to your child. Then take turns reading to each other without reading too fast or too slow. Then ask your child to do his or her best reading and read the story back to you without making any mistakes.

Grocery Shopping

Alicia looked in the refrigerator. "There is no food!" she said. 11

Her mother looked. There was some food, but no milk or bread. 23
"We will have to go shopping. Put on your coat, and get your sister," 37
she said. 39

Alicia and her sister Nicole put on their coats. They got in the car and 54
went to the store. 58

Their mother pushed the cart. Alicia looked at all of the food. There 71
were so many good things to eat. There were big red apples, bags of 85
carrots, and green beans. There was bread, cheese, and turkey. 95
There were cakes and ice cream too. 102

"I think I will make pasta for dinner," their mother said. 113

"I like pasta," Nicole replied. 118

"Me too," Alicia said. 122

"We will need pasta, sauce, and cheese. Can you help me find 134
them?" their mother asked. 138

"Yes, we can!" both girls shouted. 144

They found what they needed. Then they went home. The girls 155
helped their mother cook. 159

Directions Take turns reading the story "Grocery Shopping" aloud with your child. Read the story at least two or three times. Remind your child to pause briefly when he or she sees a comma.

The Middle of Nowhere

Ellie had heard the expression "the middle of nowhere"	9
before, but now she understood what it meant. Her parents	19
had brought Ellie and her sisters to the woods to go camping.	31
Ellie felt like she was in the middle of nowhere.	41
Mom and Dad said camping in the great outdoors would be	52
good for the kids. "I'm BORED!" Ellie whined. "There's no	62
TV, no video games, and no stores. What's there to DO out	74
here?"	75
Mom smiled. "Help us set up the tent. Then we can go hiking	88
and look for animal tracks!"	93
Ellie rolled her eyes. "Hiking is BORING," she thought.	102
Soon Ellie and her family were walking through a deep, quiet	113
forest. Ellie heard birds singing in the distance. She took	123
a deep breath of the cool, clean air. Ellie had to admit that	136
it was kind of nice in the forest. The noise of the city seemed	150
far, far away.	153
Suddenly, Ellie's mom pointed and called, "LOOK!"	160
Just a few feet away, a family of deer stood watching them.	172
Ellie stared at the beautiful animals in wonder. At last, she	183
was happy to be in the middle of nowhere.	192

School + Home

Directions Ask your child to read the story to you, showing surprise and excitement when he or she sees exclamation marks. Ask your child to emphasize words in capital letters. Then take turns reading to each other.

Curt's Birthday

Curt is excited! His birthday is Friday, and he will be seven. He is having	15
a birthday party. All of his friends are coming.	24
Curt and his friends will have fun. They will play games and watch a movie.	39
They will eat pizza and cake. Curt's mother will bake a chocolate cake.	52
That is Curt's favorite cake. Then Curt's friends will sing to him. He will	66
blow out the candles and make a wish.	74
Then it will be time for presents. "I hope I get a new book! I LOVE books,"	91
Curt says.	93
His mother laughs. "I think you might get a book. Maybe you will get a	108
game or a new shirt, too," she says.	116
"Shirts are BORING," Curt says.	121
"Is your favorite baseball shirt boring?" his mother asks.	130
Curt thinks about it. "No, a new shirt MIGHT be okay," he says.	143
"Remember to thank everyone who comes to your party. Do not be mean	156
if you do not like a present," his mother reminds him.	167
Curt nodded. "Don't worry, Mom. I will be nice, and I will say thank you."	182
"Thank you, Curt. I think the party will be fun. Will you help me bake	197
the cake?" his mother asks.	202
"Yes!"	203

Directions Take turns reading the story "Curt's Birthday" aloud with your child. Then have your child practice reading it, emphasizing words in capital letters. Make sure your child shows excitement or surprise when he or she reads an exclamation mark.

Fluency Lesson 4

Rate 2 **25**

Hot Rod

Dad got Dan a hot rod.   6

Dan got in it.   10

Kim can hop in it.   15

Pat and Nan hop in it.   21

Can Dot pop in it?   26

Can Mac fit in it?   31

They can fit.   34

They got in.   37

The hot rod cannot go.   42

Did Dad get gas?   46

School + Home **Directions** Read the story "Hot Rod" to your child using your normal rate of speaking. Pay particular attention to reading each word correctly. Then ask your child to read the story at the same speed used when he or she talks and without making any mistakes.

Fluency Lesson 5

On the Playground

Every day	2
we run and play.	6
I like to jump rope.	11
Trisha likes to swing.	15
Mike plays kick ball.	19
May runs races with Liz.	24
We all play hide and seek.	30
We hide. Jess seeks.	34
I hide under the slide.	39
She finds me!	42
Now I'm it.	45

School + Home **Directions** Read the story "On the Playground" to your child. Then have your child practice reading the story with you at a normal pace.

Sand Fun

The sun is hot.   4
Tim gets us a spot on the   11
hot sand.   13
Quick! Pam has a mat for   19
us to sit on.   23

Bob has big pots and pans.   29
Look! He digs up sand.   34
Pam and Deb fill the pots and   41
pans with sand.   44

Tim dumps sand and pats it.   50
Pam adds rocks.   53
Deb adds a flag on top!   59

Will we win?   62
A man picks the best one.   68
We win!   70

Directions Read the story "Sand Fun" to your child in your normal speaking voice. Then have your child read it back to you until he or she can read it without making any mistakes.

At the Airport

Dan is going on a trip!	6
His family is visiting	10
his grandmother.	12
Dan's father carries their bags.	17
A woman takes their bags.	22
She puts them on a cart.	28
Dan waits in a long line.	34
Then he takes off his shoes.	40
He walks through	43
the metal detector.	46
Dan puts his shoes on.	51
Dan's family sits at the gate.	57
Dan looks at the planes.	62
They are big!	65
Then they get in line again.	71
It is time to	75
get on the plane!	79

School + Home **Directions** Take turns reading the story "At the Airport" aloud with your child. Read the story at least two or three times. Remind your child to read every word and read it correctly. If your child skips words, have him or her track the print.

Name _____

Jack's Trip

Jack and his cat plan a camping trip.	8
Jack gets a map.	12
Jack lets Cat pick the	17
best spots to hike and camp.	23
Jack must pack his bag.	28
He packs cat snacks and	33
sandwiches.	34
He packs extra socks	38
and a fishing pole.	42
Cat is ready to go!	47
Jack has his bag on his back.	54
Cat jumps on the bag on	60
Jack's back!	62
Jack and Cat walk up a hill	69
and through a forest.	73
They walk by a river	78
and over a bridge.	82
It's snack time!	85
Jack and Cat sit on a rock.	92
They eat their snacks together.	97
Jack and Cat like to go	103
on trips!	105

 School + Home **Directions** Read the story "Jack's Trip" to your child, and have your child practice reading it. Then ask your child to read the story to you without making any mistakes.

Our Solar System

We live on Earth. Earth is a planet.   8

There are eight planets   12

in our solar system.   16

Earth is the third planet.   21

It is not the biggest planet.   27

The biggest planet is Jupiter.   32

It is not the smallest planet.   38

The smallest planet is Mercury.   43

Earth has one moon.   47

Some planets do not have moons.   53

Jupiter has 63 moons!   57

The planets go around the Sun.   63

The Sun is a star.   68

It is very hot   72

and very bright.   75

The Sun makes our planet warm   81

and our days bright.   85

Many other stars shine   89

in our night sky.   93

Directions Read the story to your child with no mistakes in your normal speaking voice. Then ask your child to read the story correctly without reading too fast or too slow.

Bob's New Dog

Why is Bob so happy? It is his birthday. He has a pretty   13
new dog.   15

"My dog has red fur. I will name her Penny," Bob says.   27

Dad and Bob get a soft, blue bed for Penny. "We will put   40
Penny's bed in a quiet spot."   46

Mom and Bob get two bowls for Penny. Bob fills one bowl   58
with water. He puts food in the other bowl. Penny eats three   70
times a day. She is still growing.   77

Then Bob takes Penny to the vet.   84

"Penny is growing big and strong," the vet says. "Now you   95
can walk her outside every day."   101

Bob loves Penny. "You are my best friend," he says. Penny   112
is a happy dog. Bob is a happy boy.   121

School + Home **Directions** Read the story to your child in your normal speaking voice. Then ask your child to read the story without reading too fast or too slow.

Allie's Art

Allie makes art. She likes to paint, and she likes to draw.   12

Allie draws pictures. She draws trees and squirrels. She   21
draws her school and flowers on a hill. She draws her   32
brother and sister.   35

Allie paints with a brush. She paints a garden. The grass   46
is green, and the ground is brown. The water is blue. The   58
sun is yellow, and the flowers are red.   66

Allie draws a picture for her mother. It is a brown cat. The   79
cat sits in a chair. Her mother likes the picture.   89

Allie paints at school too. The children paint a picture on   100
the wall. The picture shows a bus. The bus is yellow. There   112
are children on the bus. They wave good-bye.   120

School + Home **Directions** Read the story "Allie's Art" to your child. Then have your child practice reading the story with you at a normal pace.

Cats!

How are a baby tiger and a little kitten the same? Both 12
animals are cats! Tigers and kittens are different too. You 22
can have a pet cat. You cannot have a tiger in your house. 35

There are many kinds of cats. Some cats have long hair. 46
Others have short hair. Some cats have blue eyes. Other 56
cats have green, yellow, or brown eyes. 63

All cats can climb trees. They run very fast, and they can 75
jump high in the air. They walk quietly on their soft paws. 87
Many cats catch their own food. 93

Why are cats so special? Cats have very good hearing. 103
They also make many different sounds. A happy cat will 113
purr, but an angry cat will hiss loudly. Did a cat ever say 126
"Meow!" to you? That friendly cat was saying hello. 135

Cats are good pets. They can be good friends too! 145

School + Home **Directions** Read the story "Cats!" to your child. Then have your child practice reading the story until he or she can read it without skipping or substituting any words.

Baking Cookies

Making cookies is easy and fun. You can make cookies too! 11
Your parents can help you. A recipe will tell you what to do. 24

First, you need a big bowl and a spoon. Get butter and eggs. 37
You will also need sugar, flour, baking soda, salt, and vanilla. 48
Check the recipe. Then measure what you need. 56

Stir together the butter and sugar. Then crack the eggs. Do 67
not get any shells in the bowl! Stir in the eggs. Add the vanilla. 81
Stir it up. Add the flour, salt, and baking soda. Stir it up again. 95

Then roll the dough into balls. Put the balls on a pan. Ask 108
your parents to bake the dough for ten minutes. Soon you 119
can eat a cookie! 123

Share your cookies. It feels good to share. 131

You can cook other food too. Make sure you ask for help. 143
It is important to be safe when you cook. 152

School + Home

Directions Take turns reading the story "Baking Cookies" aloud with your child. Read the story at least two or three times. Remind your child to read every word and read it correctly. If your child skips words, have him or her track the print.

Moving Day

It's moving day for Enzo and his family. His brother and sister   12
have been carrying boxes into their new house all afternoon.   22
Their dog Dora runs from room to room wagging her tail.   33

"There are empty boxes everywhere! I can't see the   42
bedroom floor!" calls Enzo's mother from upstairs. "Enzo,   50
please take these boxes to the garage. Remember that it's   60
your job to watch Dora. Make sure she doesn't get outdoors   71
and get lost."   74

Just then, Dora races downstairs, through the front doorway,   83
across the yard, and down the street. Enzo follows, calling   93
Dora's name. But Dora is nowhere in sight. "I hope Dora   104
isn't lost," Enzo says to himself. "That would be terrible!"   114

At that minute, a boy walks from behind a small house down   126
the block. He is carrying Dora in his arms. "Is this your   138
dog?" he asks Enzo. "I found her exploring my backyard.   148
My name is Abe. I hope you'll be going to my school this   161
year. What's your name?"   165

All at once, Enzo feels right at home on his new street.   177

Directions Read the story to your child in your normal speaking voice. Be sure to pause at appropriate places and to group words naturally. Then challenge your child to practice reading the story to you without making any mistakes.

Soccer Game

Dan and James are on a soccer team. Their team is called   12
the Bears. They practice twice a week and play games every   23
Saturday morning.   25

The most important rule in soccer is not to touch the ball   37
with your hands. The goalie defends the goal. He is allowed   48
to use his hands, but everyone else has to use their feet,   60
knees, and heads. Dan likes hitting the ball with his head.   71
James likes to play goalie.   76

The Bears are playing the Giants. The Giants have the ball   87
at the start of the game. James is defending the Bears' goal.   99
He stands in front of the goal and watches the ball. A Giants   112
player kicks the ball down toward the goal.   120

James waves his arms. The Giants player kicks the ball hard   131
toward the right side of the goal. James dives and catches   142
it! He gets up and throws the ball to Dan.   152

Dan starts kicking the ball down the field toward the other   163
goal. He runs fast, kicking the ball ahead. Then Dan kicks   174
the ball hard toward the goal. The goalie dives and misses.   185
Goal!   186

Directions Read the story to your child in your normal speaking voice. Be sure to show excitement when you read the word with an exclamation mark. Then ask your child to read the story correctly without reading too fast or too slow.

First Day of School

Why is Tim excited? Today he is going to school.	10
Tim has a new bag to hold books. He has a new	22
lunch box too!	25
Tim's mother walks Tim to school. The school is only a	36
few blocks away. Tim sees his friends while he walks.	46
Tim's mother walks with him to the classroom. Tim walks	56
into the room and finds his desk. This will be fun!	67

School + Home **Directions** Read the story to your child in your normal speaking voice. Then ask your child to read the story without reading too fast or too slow.

Fluency Lesson 7

Name _____

Yard Work

Nick likes to help his mom and dad.	8
He helps work in the yard.	14
Dad mows the grass.	18
Nick pulls weeds.	21
Mom plants flowers.	24
Nick digs the holes.	28
Dad trims the trees.	32
Nick carries the branches.	36
Mom picks the flowers.	40
Nick puts them in a vase.	46
Dad paints the fence.	50
Nick paints too!	53
Mom waters the garden.	57
Nick waters plants too!	61

School + Home **Directions** Read the story "Yard Work" to your child. Then have your child practice reading the story with you at a normal pace.

Buddy

Buddy is my dog. Buddy is a very smart dog.   10
Buddy does tricks!   13

Buddy can sit up. Buddy can roll over   21
in the grass. Buddy can run and jump   29
in the pond. Buddy does tricks!   35

One day Buddy got sick. Buddy's skin   42
was hot. He would not play with me.   50
Dad took Buddy to the vet. The vet   58
will fix Buddy!   61

Buddy is back! He runs in the sun. He sits   71
and rolls over in the grass. Buddy does tricks!   80

School + Home **Directions** Have your child practice reading the story "Buddy" to you until he or she can read it without any mistakes and in a way that sounds like natural speech.

Name _____

The Moon

The Moon shines in the night sky. The Moon goes   10
around Earth.   12

The Moon is not like Earth. It has no air. People cannot live   25
on the Moon.   28

The Moon has deserts, mountains, and valleys. It also has   38
craters. Craters are holes where rocks hit the Moon.   47

People wanted to go to the Moon. People made space   57
ships. They went into space. In 1969, a space ship landed   68
on the Moon. Neil Armstrong walked there. He put a flag   79
on the Moon.   82

School + Home

Directions Take turns reading the story "The Moon" aloud with your child. Read the story at least two or three times. Remind your child to read every word and read it correctly. If your child skips words, have him or her track the print.

A New Friend

Turtle liked swimming in the pond on the farm, but he didn't
have any friends to play with him. He was all alone.

One day he saw a little white cat. "Oh no! I can't swim.
How can I cross the pond?" Cat asked.

"Jump on my back, and I'll carry you across the pond,"
said Turtle.

So Cat jumped on Turtle's back, and together they crossed
the pond.

"Thank you," Cat said. "Now we can go to the party with
my friends."

There were many animals at the party. Everyone was
dancing and having a good time.

Turtle made lots of new friends at the party and was never
alone again.

	12
	23
	36
	44
	55
	57
	67
	69
	81
	83
	92
	98
	110
	112

Directions Read the story to your child in your normal speaking voice. Then ask
your child to read it aloud. Take turns with your child reading the parts of the different
characters in the story. Then ask your child to read the story alone without making any
mistakes.

Trucks

There are many kinds of trucks. Pick-up trucks and mail   10
trucks are small trucks. Small trucks are good for moving   20
small loads. They can also tow boats and campers. Some   30
people drive small trucks every day.   36

Big trucks do big jobs. Garbage trucks, tow trucks, and fire   47
trucks are all big trucks. Street sweepers and snow plows   57
are big trucks too.   61

Another big truck is a tractor-trailer, or big rig. You see big   73
rigs on the highway. These big trucks pull a long trailer   84
behind them. They have 18 wheels! Some trailers hold food.   94
Others hold computers or car parts. Big rigs can also   104
pull mobile homes or big trailers with nine cars on them!   115

School + Home

Directions Read the story to your child in your normal speaking voice. Be sure to show excitement when you read words with an exclamation mark. Then ask your child to read the story correctly without reading too fast or too slow.

Name _____

Cool!

It was a hot day. Liz and her family went to the zoo. A man   15
was feeding the dolphins. They eat little fish.   23

"What would you like to know about dolphins?" he asked.   33

"What do dolphins like to do?" asked Liz.   41

"Dolphins like to play," the man said. "They jump out of the   53
water into the air. They play in the waves. Young dolphins   64
play together. They play for hours."   70

Three dolphins leaped into the air. They hit the water with a   82
splash. Liz's family got all wet.   88

"Cool!" Liz said. She was happy.   94

School + Home **Directions** Read the story to your child in your normal speaking voice. Then ask your child to read the story without reading too fast or too slow.

44 Accuracy and Rate 4   **Fluency Lesson 8**

Copyright © Pearson Education, Inc., or its affiliates. All Rights Reserved.

The Pumpkin Patch

Mrs. Lopez's class is on a field trip! They are at the pumpkin   13
patch. They have a lot of fun! They take a hay ride.   25

They pick out pumpkins to take home. There are little   35
pumpkins and big pumpkins. Some are orange, and some   44
are white. Some are round, and some are tall. Bill picks a   56
big round pumpkin. Jim picks a little orange pumpkin.   65

There is a petting zoo too! Jaden pets a goat. Alex and Bill   78
pet the rabbits. Jim and Maria feed the chickens. Bill feeds   89
ducks.   90

Then the class sits down for lunch. They have chicken,   100
apples, and carrots. Mrs. Lopez has a surprise for them.   110
There is pumpkin pie too! Maria smiles. She loves pie.   120

School + Home **Directions** Read the story "The Pumpkin Patch" to your child. Then have your child practice reading the story with you at a normal pace.

Apples

There are many kinds of apples. They can be large or small.   12
Apples can be many colors. Each kind of apple has a special   24
name too. Gala apples are sweet, red, and yellow. Granny   34
Smith apples are green. One sweet apple is called Pink Lady.   45
It is pink and yellow! The name Honeycrisp tells you how   56
these apples taste and feel!   61

Farmers grow all apples in the same way. They plant young   72
trees in long rows. The young trees need a lot of water and   85
light. In a few years, apples will grow on the new trees. Then   98
farmers pick apples from the trees. The apples are shipped   108
to stores. Then you can buy the apples! There are many   119
ways to eat apples. People cook apples in pies. Other   129
people eat apples on their own. How do you eat apples?   140
What kinds do you eat?   145

School + Home **Directions** Read the story to your child in your normal speaking voice. Then ask your child to read the story correctly without reading too fast or too slow.

Swimming Lessons

Rosa and Ana take swimming lessons. They go to the pool at   12
the park. Rosa likes the pool. The water is cool. There is   24
a diving board in the deep end of the pool. Rosa wants to   37
learn how to dive too.   42

They have lessons every week. Rosa likes the lessons. Ana   52
was scared at first. Now she likes to swim too.   62

First, their teacher showed them how to blow bubbles. Then   72
they learned how to hold their breath. Ana was scared. She   83
did not like it. Her mother helped her feel better.   93

Next, they learned how to float. Then they learned how to   104
kick. Ana likes to kick. Then the teacher showed them how   115
to use their arms.   119

Rosa was surprised. She could swim! Soon Ana could   128
swim too. Their mother was very proud. They swim all the   139
time. Rosa and Ana love their swimming lessons. Next   148
week Rosa will learn how to dive!   155

Directions Read the story to your child in your normal speaking voice. Be sure to show excitement when you read words with an exclamation mark. Then ask your child to read the story correctly without reading too fast or too slow.

A Room Full of Music

Today there will be a big party in Zack's class. The children	12
want to sing and dance, but there is no music.	22

"How can we have our party without music?" asks Zack.	32
"We can still have games, but we won't be able to sing and	45
dance. That's no fun!"	49

"I know," says Marco. "We can make our own music with	60
things in this room."	64

"Marco is right," Valerie says. "We can make music with	74
almost anything! We can tap our hands on different parts of	85
that big trash can to play different notes."	93

"What a wonderful idea!" says Mrs. Diggs, their teacher.	102
"You can also put a tight string around a box. When you	114
snap the string, it will make a good beat to keep time to the	128
trash can's sound."	131

Soon Zack is snapping out a strong beat with the string	142
on the box. Valerie bangs a song on the big trash can.	154
The children sing and clap along with the music and have	165
a wonderful party!	168

School + Home

Directions Read the story to your child in your normal speaking voice. Be sure to pause at appropriate places and to group words naturally. Then challenge your child to practice reading the story to you without making any mistakes.

Texas

People say, "Everything is bigger in Texas." Texas is big! It is   12
about 800 miles wide. Four Minnesotas would fit inside Texas.   22

Some parts of Texas get snow in the winter. Other parts are   34
warmer. Sometimes the weather is scary. Texas can have   43
a lot of bad storms. Some parts of Texas have tornadoes   54
in the summer.   57

Many people live in Texas. Some people live on farms   67
or ranches. Farmers work very hard. They grow crops like   77
wheat. Ranchers take care of sheep and cows. There   86
are 12 million cows in Texas! Can you believe that?   96

Many people live in big cities too. Houston is the biggest   107
city in Texas. More than 5 million people live in and around   119
Houston.   120

Another big city is Austin. Austin is the state capital. Austin   131
has a big music fest every year. San Antonio is a big city   144
too. It is the home of the Alamo. During the Texas   155
Revolution, a big battle happened there. People still say,   164
"Remember the Alamo!"   167

School + Home

Directions Take turns reading the story "Texas" aloud with your child. Read the story at least two or three times. Remind your child to read every word and read it correctly. If your child has trouble reading certain words, read them aloud first. Then have your child read the words with and without you.

Monday Morning

At her house, Ruby gets on the bus.	8
She talks with friends.	12
At school, the bell rings.	17
Ruby goes inside.	20
In the classroom, Ruby hangs up her bag.	28
She puts away her lunch box.	34
At her desk, Ruby opens her book.	41
She loves to read.	45

School + Home

Directions Read the story to your child. Make sure to pause briefly for commas. Then ask your child to read the story. Make sure your child reads in a natural way and not word-by-word.

Name _____

Robin's Nest

In the spring, the bird builds a nest.   8
She uses sticks and grass.   13

In the nest, she lays four eggs.   20
The little eggs are blue.   25

She keeps the eggs warm.   30
After two weeks, the eggs hatch.   36

The baby birds have no feathers.   42
As they grow, they grow feathers.   48

After two weeks, they can fly!   54

Directions Read the story "Robin's Nest" to your child, pausing briefly for each comma. Then have your child practice reading the story with you at a normal pace.

Lake Cake

Mom, Dad, and Jake live by a lake. Jake likes to fish. Mom   13
likes to bake.   16

Mom says, "I will bake a blue cake. I will call it a lake cake."   31
Jake wants to fish, but Jake likes cake.   39

"I will stay and help bake!" says Jake.   47

Jake mixes the cake. Oh, no! Jake mixes too fast!   57
Jake makes a mess.   61

Mom and Jake laugh. Then they clean up the mess.   71

Directions Read the story "Lake Cake" to your child, grouping the words appropriately.
Then ask your child to read the story to you with correct phrasing.

Jenna's Bike

Jenna has a new bike. Her bike is green. It has a basket on   14
the front. The basket has flowers on it!   22

Every afternoon, Jenna rides her bike. She rides up and   32
down the street. She wears a helmet. It is green too!   43

Jenna rides with her friends, Charlotte and Sarah. Jenna's   52
sister, Zoey, wants to ride too.   58

Jenna's mother says, "You are too little, Zoey. When you   68
are big, you can ride a bike."   75

School + Home

Directions Take turns reading the story "Jenna's Bike" aloud with your child. Read the story at least two or three times. Remind your child to pause briefly when he or she sees a comma.

Andy and the Lion

One day, Andy was walking through the forest. Far away, he   11
heard crying. He walked until he got closer to the sound.   22

Through the trees, Andy saw a lion lying on the ground. The   34
lion was crying.   37

Andy was scared. Lions scare people!   43

The lion looked up and saw Andy. "Don't go! I won't   54
hurt you," the lion said.   59

Slowly, Andy walked up to the lion. "Why are you crying?"   70
he asked.   72

The lion held up his big, furry paw. There was a thorn stuck   85
in it. "This hurts," the lion said.   92

"Oh, I can fix that," Andy said. He quickly pulled out   103
the thorn.   105

"Thank you!" said the lion.   110

Sometimes even a lion needs help!   116

Directions Read the story to your child, pausing when you see a comma. Be sure to show excitement when you read words with an exclamation mark. Then ask your child to read the story correctly with appropriate phrasing.

Snow Day

When Michelle woke up, it was snowing. She brushed her   10
teeth and got dressed. Michelle needed to eat breakfast,   19
pack her lunch, and put on her coat, hat, and gloves.   30

She walked down the stairs to the kitchen.   38

Michelle's mother stood at the stove, making pancakes   46
and bacon. "Good morning!" she said.   52

Michelle's sister, Jenny, sat at the table. She was wearing   62
pajamas. "Mom, Jenny isn't dressed!" she said, pointing.   70

"Oh, I know. It's a snow day, and all the schools are closed," 83
Michelle's mother said.   86

"Cool! Can we go sledding later?" Michelle asked.   94

"Maybe, if you clean your room first," Michelle's mother   103
answered.   104

"I'll clean my room, Mom," Jenny said.   111

"Me too! I'll do it right after breakfast," Michelle said with 122
a smile.   124

Directions Read the story to your child in your normal speaking voice with appropriate phrasing. Then ask your child to read it aloud. Remind your child to pause briefly for commas and pause longer for periods.

Luca's New Bike

Luca needed money to buy a bike, but he did not want to   13
work. Luca felt lazy.   17

He looked for money on the street. He only found one penny!   29

His dad smiled at him. Dad said, "Son, do some work! Then   41
you can make money for a new bike."   49

The next day Luca went to work. He walked his neighbor's   60
big yellow dog. He cut the grass in his front and back yards.   73
When Luca was done, he was very tired!   81

For many weeks, Luca worked hard. He saved all his money.   92
At last, he had enough money to buy a bike.   102

Luca and Dad walked to the bike store. But Luca did not   114
walk home. He rode his new red bike.   122

School + Home

Directions Read the story as if you were talking to your child. Then have your child practice reading the story in a natural voice and at a normal pace. Encourage your child to pause briefly for each comma and to group words.

Name _____

Robots Explore the Ocean

There is more water on Earth than land. The oceans on Earth   12
are huge. The oceans are very deep. They are also very cold.   24

We can explore some parts of the oceans. Others are too   35
deep. Robots are used to explore the oceans. Robots can   45
go into very deep water. They do not need air or food. They   58
don't feel cold.   61

The robots can "see" in the water. It is very dark in the ocean.   75
Robots use bright lights to see plants and animals. They see   86
mountains. They see many kinds of fish. Some fish light   96
up! There is a lot to see in the ocean.   106

Without robots, we would not know what lives deep under   116
the water. There are many places to explore. Robots can   126
see them all.   129

Directions Read the story "Robots Explore the Ocean" to your child. Then have your child practice reading the story with you, pausing briefly for commas.

Name _____

Helping Grandfather

It is very early, but Shawn and Ronna are dressed and ready   12
to go. Today they will visit Grandfather. He lives in another   23
town. They will help him make bread. He loves to cook, and   35
they love to help.   39

Their mother takes them to Grandfather's house. When he   48
sees Shawn and Ronna, Grandfather smiles. "Thank you for   57
coming!" he says. "Let's start cooking!"   63

First, the children wash their hands. Next, they mix flour,   73
milk, and eggs. Their grandfather adds butter and salt.   82

What happens next? Shawn and Ronna mix everything   90
together. Then Grandfather puts the bread mix into a pan   100
and bakes it. It smells so good! After the bread is done,   112
Grandfather lets it cool.   116

Shawn and Ronna like to make bread. They like to eat it   128
even more! Ronna puts honey on her bread. Grandfather's   137
bread is the best. They make more bread to take home.   148
Their mother loves it too!   153

School + Home **Directions** Read the story "Helping Grandfather" to your child, grouping the words
appropriately. Then ask your child to read the story to you and group words in a way that
sounds natural and makes sense.

Name _____

Camping Trip

My family likes to go camping. We go camping every year,   11
and we always go to the same place. We go to a lake. It is   26
deep, cold, and full of big, fast fish.   34

My cousins come too. We like to play together. We walk in   46
the woods, and we pick flowers. We swim in the lake. Early in   59
the morning, we go fishing with our dads.   67

My family sleeps in a big blue tent. My uncle and cousins   79
sleep in their own tent. We cook our food over a fire. We   92
cook lots of good food. If we catch fish, we cook those too.   105
Then we sing songs, and we all go to sleep.   115

Sometimes we see animals. Last year, we saw a big brown   126
bear. It wanted our food. We see birds all the time. My   138
mother asks us not to feed the birds, but that is hard. I like   152
feeding the birds.   155

After a week, we go home. But we will camp next year!   167

Directions Take turns reading the story "Camping Trip" aloud with your child. Read the story at least two or three times. Remind your child to pause briefly when he or she sees a comma.

A Big Game for Everyone!

It's spring, and every day the children in Trini's class play	11
kickball. They play together on the school playground. Trini	20
and Michael want to play on their class team, so they	31
work hard.	33

"We run and practice kicking the ball every day. We are	44
getting better and better!" Trini says.	50

"Maybe our new teacher, Mr. Ramos, will let us play on our	62
class team," Michael says.	66

The next day, Mr. Ramos talks to the class about the first	78
big game. "I have a surprise for you. Because so many	89
children want to play, there will be two teams, not one,"	100
says Mr. Ramos.	103

When they hear the news, all the children clap. Now no one	115
will be left out. Everyone in the class will be able to play on	129
one of the two teams.	134

"I want you all to listen, so I can tell you some more good	148
news," says Mr. Ramos. "Our class teams will be playing in	159
the park near our school. The first big game will be in two	172
weeks. Work hard so you will be ready!"	180

Directions As you read the story to your child, pause at commas to group words together in phrases. Then have your child practice reading the story to you in the same way.

Dwayne's Birthday Surprise

Today is Dwayne's birthday. He hurries home from school. He looks   11
for a letter from his friend Duncan. For two years, Dwayne and   23
Duncan have been pen pals. Duncan said he is sending a special   35
surprise for Dwayne's birthday.   39

Duncan lives on a farm in another state. In his letters, Duncan writes   52
about his life on the farm, far away from city life. He writes about   66
where his family lives and how he loves to read on the long   79
bus ride to school. Duncan says he hopes to visit a big city someday.   93

Dwayne writes about his life in the city. There he rides the subway   106
train to school. He writes about his favorite songs and the piano   118
lessons he takes every week.   123

"There is no letter from Duncan today," Dwayne tells his father sadly.   135
"He forgot my birthday."   139

"I think you might hear from Duncan very soon," Dwayne's father   150
says, smiling.   152

Just then, the doorbell rings. Dwayne opens the door, and there is   164
Duncan!   165

"Happy birthday!" Duncan shouts.   169

"Wow!" says Dwayne. "What a great surprise!"   176

Directions Read "Dwayne's Birthday Surprise" to your child, paying attention to reading groups of words together in phrases that make sense. Then have your child practice reading the story. Challenge your child to read the entire story without making mistakes.

Name _____

My Brother

I have a big brother.   5
His name is Roberto.   9

Roberto is 14 years old,   14
and he is my best friend.   20

We have fun together.   24
Roberto plays catch with me,   29
and he takes me fishing.   34

Every morning, Roberto makes   38
my breakfast. Then he walks   43
with me to school.   47

Walking Dogs

I have two dogs, Max and Bella.	7
They are good dogs.	11
Every afternoon, I walk my dogs.	17
Max is a big brown dog.	23
Bella is a little black dog.	29
After school, I put on their leashes.	36
Then we go outside.	40
We walk down the street. I am careful.	48
I watch for cars, bikes, and people.	55

Directions Read the story "Walking Dogs" to your child, pausing briefly for each comma. Pause longer at each period. Then have your child practice reading the story with you. Make sure your child groups words in a way that sounds natural and makes sense.

School + Home

A Clean Room

Julie likes to help her parents. Julie keeps her room clean. 11

"Thank you for your help," Julie's mother says. 19

Every morning, Julie makes her bed. Then she helps her 29
little sister, Sandy, make her bed too. 36

Once a week, Julie cleans her room. First, she puts away 47
her toys. Next, she puts her books away. Last, Julie helps 58
her mother vacuum the room. Julie is glad to help. 68

School + Home **Directions** Read the story "A Clean Room" to your child, grouping the words appropriately. Then ask your child to read the story to you with correct phrasing.

Fire Drill

Willy's school had a fire drill.   6

When the bell rang, Willy's class lined up by the door. They   18
lined up in pairs. Willy walked with his friend, Alex.   28

Their teacher, Mrs. Sanchez, walked with them down   36
the hall. Other classes walked with them.   43

The bell was loud! It hurt Willy's ears. He was glad to   55
get outside.   57

They walked to the fence. The bell stopped.   65

"Now we can go inside," Mrs. Sanchez said.   73

School + Home

Directions Tell your child to read the story silently before reading aloud. Then take turns reading the story "Fire Drill" aloud with your child. Read the story at least two or three times.

Fourth of July

Today is the Fourth of July. We are going to the park.   12

First, we will watch the parade. There will be bands,   22
floats, and horses. The bands will march and play music.   32

Next, we will eat dinner. I will eat hot dogs, corn, and beans.   45
Yum!   46

After dark, we will watch the fireworks. They shoot up   56
into the sky. Boom! Boom! Fireworks are loud and bright.   66

Red, white, blue fireworks explode. Pink hearts, yellow stars,   75
and purple flowers burn in the night sky.   83

School + Home **Directions** Read the story to your child. Pause briefly when you see a comma. Be sure to show excitement when you read an exclamation mark. Then ask your child to read the story correctly in the same way.

Tigers

Tigers are amazing animals. They are big cats, like lions and   11
cheetahs. They have orange fur with black and white stripes.   21
Every tiger has a different pattern of stripes.   29

Tigers eat animals, both large and small. They hunt at   39
night and sleep during the day. Tigers can weigh up to   50
500 pounds. They roar so loud that you can hear it two   62
miles away.   64

Tigers live in Asia in both cold and warm areas. Unlike   75
other big cats, tigers love to swim. They always live near   86
water. Except for mothers and cubs, tigers live alone.   95
Tigers may live up to 27 years.   102

School + Home

Directions Read the story to your child in your normal speaking voice. Then ask your child to read it aloud. Remind your child to pause briefly for commas and pause longer after periods.

The Street Fair

Eddie's neighbors are excited. There is a street fair today.	10
There are no cars on the street. Instead, many people walk	21
down the street in the bright spring light.	29
In the morning, Eddie and Maya go to the fair. What do	41
they find?	43
Some people sell food from different countries. Other	51
people sell beautiful clothes, games, and books. A band	60
plays music, and people sing and dance.	67
"Let's buy our lunch now," Eddie says to Maya.	76
"Good idea! Then I will buy a gift for my sister," Maya says.	89
After lunch, Eddie and Maya stay at the fair. They sing	100
and dance with their neighbors. No one wants this day	110
to end!	112

School + Home **Directions** Read the story to your child at a normal rate of speed. Pause briefly for commas. Then have your child read the story in the same way without any mistakes.

Amy's New Pet

Amy wants a pet. Every day she asks her mother for a pet.   13
Every day her mother says, "No."   19

First, Amy wants a dog. "Oh, please, Mom! Can I have   30
a dog? I will take good care of it. I will take it for walks. I will   47
feed it, give it water, and brush it," Amy says.   57

"Will you clean up after it?" her mother asks.   66

After that, Amy decides that she does not want a dog.   77
She wants a cat or maybe a rabbit.   85

Again, her mother asks, "Will you clean up after it?"   95

Amy thinks hard. "Maybe I want a mouse, a bird, or a fish."   108

"They all need to keep clean," her mother says.   117

"I will clean up after it," Amy says.   125

"Then we will go look for a pet tomorrow," her mother says.   137

Directions Read the story "Amy's New Pet" to your child, pausing briefly for each comma. Then have your child practice reading the story with you. Make sure your child groups words in a way that sounds natural and makes sense.

The Lion and the Mouse

One day a lion was asleep in the grass. Then a mouse   12
ran by. He ran right across the lion's face! With a loud roar,   25
the lion woke up. He picked up the mouse with his big paw.   38

"Please do not eat me!" cried the tiny mouse. "Let me go,   50
and one day I will help YOU!"   57

"How can YOU help ME?" said the lion, laughing. "I am   68
the most important animal in the world! I do not need you."   80

But the lion was kind. He let the mouse go free.   91

On the next day, the lion fell into a big net. "Oh no! If I   106
cannot get away, the hunters will kill me!" cried the lion.   117

By chance, the tiny mouse ran by. He saw the lion. Right   129
away, the little mouse started biting the net. His sharp teeth   140
cut the net.   143

"You see, I was right after all," said the mouse. "Even a tiny   156
mouse can help a big lion."   162

School + Home **Directions** Read the story "The Lion and the Mouse" to your child. Then have your child practice reading the story. Make sure your child pauses briefly for commas and groups words in a way that sounds natural.

Checkers

Name _____

Do you know how to play checkers? I do. It is easy and a   14
lot of fun!   17

I play checkers with my brother Van. Checkers is a board   28
game. It has round pieces called checkers. I move the red   39
pieces, and Van moves the black pieces. We each have   49
12 pieces.   51

The board has dark squares and light squares, but pieces   61
only move on dark squares. We take turns moving pieces.   71

There are rules. We can only move to an empty square.   82
Can we jump over squares? If Van's piece is on a square,   94
I can try to jump it. If there is an empty square on the other   109
side, my piece can move there. Then I take Van's piece off   121
the board.   123

How do I win? I jump over all of Van's pieces. Checkers   135
looks easy, but it can be hard to win. I have to watch Van.   149
It is easy to make a mistake. Even if I do not win, checkers   163
is fun. I might win next time! Let's play!   172

Directions Tell your child to read the story silently before reading aloud. Then take turns reading the story "Checkers" aloud with your child. Read the story together at least two or three times. Encourage your child to pause briefly for commas, pause longer for periods, and group words in a way that sounds natural.

Hen's New Clothes

Hen wanted to buy new clothes, but she had only a few coins.	13
"I will go to the market and see what I can find!" said Hen.	27
At the market, Hen's few coins would not even buy one shoe. So	40
she bought a yellow basket to wear as a hat and a purple blanket	54
to wear as a dress. Hen spent her last coin on a piece of rope.	69
"This rope makes a fine belt!" said Hen happily.	78
After Hen flew back to the farm, she put on her new clothes to	92
show Rooster and Donkey. Rooster and Donkey just stared.	101
"That basket on your head is very yellow," said Rooster at last.	113
"And that blanket you have tied on with a rope is very purple," said	127
Donkey.	128
"But don't I look beautiful in my new clothes?" asked Hen.	139
"If you ask me, a basket is for collecting eggs," said Rooster.	151
"And if you ask me, a blanket is for making a bed," said Donkey.	165
"Well, I think I look just fine!" said Hen. And she felt just fine, too!	180

School + Home **Directions** Read the story to your child in your normal speaking voice. Pay special attention to grouping words. Then ask your child to practice reading the story to you in the same way and without making mistakes.

Down at the Creek

Jacob lives near a creek. A creek is a small river. The creek   13
is one of his favorite places. Jacob and his friends, Mike and   25
Danny, go to the creek after school.   32

The creek runs through the woods behind Jacob's house.   41
The woods are full of tall trees, birds, and small animals.   52
Sometimes the boys see deer when they walk through the   62
woods.   63

On warm days, the boys take off their shoes and splash   74
in the water. They skip little rocks across the water, look for   86
frogs, and climb trees. Sometimes they play hide and seek,   96
and they try to catch fish.   102

Since the boys spend so much time at the creek, Jacob's   113
dad wants to help them. He thinks that they need a fort.   125
Jacob's dad buys some wood and nails. With help from the   136
boys, he clears away the bushes and grass in one area.   147

First, he builds a frame for a little house. Jacob helps   158
measure the wood. His dad cuts the wood. Then Jacob   168
helps nail it together.   172

The boys help Jacob's dad set up the frame. Then they nail   184
together the walls and put on the roof. Now the boys   195
have a place to play when it rains.   203

Directions Read the story to your child in your normal speaking voice. Then ask your child to read it aloud. Remind your child to pause briefly when he or she sees commas and to pause longer after periods. Make sure your child groups words in a way that sounds natural.

Fred the Frog

Jesse has a pet frog. His name is Fred.	9
He is green with spots. Fred has webbed toes. He lives in a	22
glass box in Jesse's room. Fred says "Ribbit!"	30
Fred likes to swim! He swims in his box.	39
Fred also hops! Sometimes Jesse lets him hop	47
around the room.	50
"Ribbit! Ribbit!" says Fred as he hops.	57

School + Home

Directions Read the story to your child at a normal rate of speed. Read with feeling to make the words come alive. Then have your child read the story in the same way without making any mistakes.

The Library

Ana loves the library. She and her mother go there   10
every week.   12

Ana's mother picks out new books. She loves to read.   22

Ana likes the children's room. It has books and music. First,   33
Ana puts together a puzzle. Then she picks her new books.   44

Ana and her mother read together. They read every night.   54

School + Home **Directions** Read the story "The Library" to your child, showing feeling with your voice. Then have your child practice reading the story with you, with expression.

Whales

Whales live in the water. They jump up. They splash down. 11
They have fun! 14

Most whales are very big. Some whales are as big as a bus! 27
Some whales have teeth, and some whales do not. All 37
whales have fins. They use their fins to swim. 46

Whales have holes on top. The hole is like a nose. Whales 58
use the hole to get air. When whales go under water, the 70
hole closes. Whales like to swim and have fun! 79

Directions Read the passage "Whales" to your child at your normal rate of speaking and with feeling in your voice. Then ask your child to practice reading the passage to you with expression and without making mistakes.

Name _____

Cats

Do you have a cat? Many people have pet cats.   10

There are about 33 kinds of cats. They can have long fur or   23
short fur. Cats come in many colors. They can be white,   34
black, orange, or brown. Cats can have spots or stripes.   44

Little cats may weigh six pounds. A large cat can weigh as   56
much as 20 pounds! A cat can live for 20 years. Baby cats   69
are called kittens. A mother cat has several kittens at a time.   81

School + Home **Directions** Tell your child to read the story silently before reading aloud. Then take turns reading the story "Cats" aloud with your child. Read the story at least two or three times. Make sure your child reads with feeling.

Fun at Pine Lake

My name is Tonya. Mom, Dad, and I go to Pine Lake. I   13
skate and ride my bike. I play by the lake. Pine Lake is fun!   27

Mom and I like to walk, hike, and run at Pine Lake. We hike   41
for miles. I pick up big pine cones.   49

Dad and I dive, swim, and fish. We get lots of fish. I   62
like fish from Pine Lake!   67

At home, we eat, talk, and laugh about the day at Pine Lake.   80
That place is fun!   84

Directions Read the story "Fun at Pine Lake" to your child in your normal speaking voice and with feeling. Then ask your child to practice reading the passage in his or her normal speaking voice and to read with feeling. Challenge your child to read the story once without any mistakes.

Name _____

Thanksgiving

My favorite holiday is Thanksgiving. We go to my grandma's   10
house. The whole family comes to visit.   17

I get to play with my cousins. We like to dress up in old   31
clothes and put on plays for our family. My cousin Sarah   42
likes to sing songs, and we dance behind her.   51

All the parents help in the kitchen. We sneak in and eat bits   64
of food when they aren't looking.   70

My mother makes her famous pumpkin pie. My uncle cooks   80
a turkey outside. My grandma makes her special potatoes   89
and gravy.   91

The potatoes are my favorite thing in the world to eat!   102

School + Home **Directions** Read the story to your child in your normal speaking voice with expression. Then ask your child to read it aloud. Remind your child to read as if he or she were speaking.

Name _____

Tom's Best Day

Tom's best friend was on vacation.   6

"What will I do? There is no one to play with today!"   18
Tom said.   20

"You can come along with me," Mom said.   28

First they washed the car in front of the house. Then they   40
went to the store to buy food. Mom got Tom his favorite   52
snack.   53

Tom flew his big red kite in the park with Mom. His kite   66
flew high in the air! Everyone stopped to watch Tom's kite.   77

"What a great kite!" a girl said to Tom. Tom and his new   90
friend played with the kite. Then he walked home with Mom.   101

"This was the best day ever!" Tom said.   109

School + Home **Directions** Read the story to your child. Then ask your child to read it with feeling. Make sure your child's voice rises and falls as he or she reads.

Fighting Fires!

Maria's job is very important. She saves people. She puts   10
out fires!   12

Maria wears special clothes to keep her safe. Today Maria   22
goes to a fire on First Street. There is a lot of smoke!   35

Maria jumps off the fire truck and picks up a long hose.   47
She holds it tight with both hands. Cold water shoots from   58
the hose.   60

It takes time, but the water puts out the fire. Now there is   73
water all over. Things are all wet!   80

No one is hurt. It will take hard work to clean up. Then   93
people can return home.   97

Now Maria can go back to the fire house and put away her   110
special fire clothes. It is time to go home.   119

School + Home

Directions Read the story "Fighting Fires!" to your child with excitement in your voice
for sentences ending in exclamation marks. Then have your child practice reading the
story in the same way.

The Farmer and the King

Long ago, a king was very sad. He was bored.   10

"I know! Today I will ride my horse into the woods and have   23
a picnic. What a smart idea!" said the king.   32

Of course, the king forgot his lunch. Then he got lost!   43

The king was very scared. He walked through the dark   53
woods and met a poor farmer. The farmer did not know the   65
king, but he shared his food with the lost man. The king ate   78
the farmer's food. He was very happy!   85

"That was good!" said the king. "You are very kind!"   95

After lunch, the king helped the farmer plant seeds. It was   106
hard work, but the king had a very good time.   116

"Working is fun!" the king said. "I would like to be a farmer   129
one day."   131

"And I would like to be a king," said the poor farmer.   143

School + Home **Directions** Read the story to your child with intonation, making your voice rise and fall as you read. Then ask your child to read it in the same way. Challenge your child to read with feeling and without making mistakes.

Help Our Earth!

Mr. Lee has an important job for his class. "We must all help 13
keep our school clean," he says. "But we will not throw 24
everything away. Let's see what we can use again. Will you 35
do your part to help our Earth?" 42

All the children want to help. First, they save old papers in 54
empty boxes. Then, they tie the papers with string. They put 65
the papers in a special blue box. 72

"Can bottles and cans be used again?" asks Gina. 81

"Yes, they can!" says Mr. Lee. "They go in the blue box too." 94

The children bring empty cans and paper every day. Soon 104
the box is full. 108

"People will use these to make new things," he says. 118

"How does using old paper again help our Earth?" 127
asks Rene. 129

"Trees are used to make paper," says Mr. Lee. "By using 140
old paper again, we can save some trees!" 148

Directions Read the story "Help Our Earth!" to your child with intonation, making
your voice rise and fall so the words sound interesting, especially when characters are
speaking. Then have your child practice reading the story in the same way. Make sure
your child reads with feeling.

Bridges Long Ago and Today

Where can you find bridges? People build bridges all over   10
the world. Bridges go up and over wide roads or across   21
water. They also go across deep places in the land. Bridges   32
stand in the country, in cities, and in the mountains, too!   43

Have you ever been on a bridge? Maybe you thought about   54
how bridges were made and how they were first used. Long   65
ago, people made some bridges from big stones. People   74
crossed these bridges by walking or riding in carts pulled by   85
horses.   86

Today we cross some of these old stone bridges in our cars.   98
In some places, stone bridges were taller than a house and   109
hundreds of miles long! Parts of these bridges still stand   119
today.   120

Why are old bridges important to us? Very old bridges   130
show us how people built things long ago. They did not   141
have the tools that we have today, but they could build   152
bridges that would last for hundreds of years!   160

Directions Read "Bridges Long Ago and Today" to your child. Try not to read too quickly or slowly. Read with expression, or feeling in your voice. Then have your child practice reading the passage in the same way. Ask your child to read the entire passage without making mistakes.

School + Home

Name _____

The Girl Who Hated Noise

Sonya hated noise. She hated it so much that she always kept   12
both hands pressed tight over her ears. "There's too much noise!"   23
Sonya yelled.   25

"A little noise could be a good thing," Father whispered. "Being   36
indoors is making you unhappy. Take Pepper for a walk to the   48
farmers' market."   50

But the market was no different. There were so many people, and   62
they were making a lot of loud noise. "I hate all noise, Pepper,"   75
Sonya said to her puppy. Pepper just barked. "Your barking is   86
hurting my ears!" Sonya howled.   91

Just then, a sack of corn fell from a cart and landed right on   105
Sonya's head. Corn was stuck in Sonya's hair, in her dress,   116
and in her ears. Sonya was so upset that she ran straight home.   129

"Home already?" Father asked. But Sonya couldn't hear anything.   138
She couldn't hear her pet parakeet chirp, and she couldn't hear her 150
favorite songs.   152

Sonya was so sad. She wanted to cry. When she bent down to   165
pet Pepper, corn fell out of her ears. Pepper barked as the corn   178
hit the floor.   181

"What a wonderful sound!" said Sonya with a big smile. "A little   193
noise CAN be a good thing!"   199

Directions Read the story to your child, allowing the volume and pitch of your voice to rise and fall naturally. Use different voices for Sonya and her father to bring the characters to life. Then ask your child to use different voices for each character as he or she practices reading the story.

Fluency Lesson 14   Expression/Intonation/Characterization 2 **85**

Name _____

Hide and Seek

James wants to play hide and seek.   7

"Will you play hide and seek with me?" James asks Tasha.   18

"No," Tasha says. "I am reading a book."   26

James asks Lee and Will to play.   33

"No," Lee says. "I am playing kickball."   40

"I will play with you!" Will says. "Can I hide first?"   51

"Yes! I will find you," James says.   58

Going to the Park

Amita likes to go to the park. She plays on	10
the swings. She digs in the sand. She goes	19
down the slide.	22
Today Amita is at home. She is bored.	30
"Can we go to the park, Dad?" she asks.	39
Dad washes dishes. "No. You can play	46
inside," he says.	49
"Why?" Amita asks.	52
"I am busy. We will go this afternoon," Dad says.	62

School + Home **Directions** Read the story "Going to the Park" with distinct voices for Amita and Dad. Then have your child practice reading the story in the same way.

The Baseball Game

Owen and his father go to a baseball game.   9

They show a man their tickets. "Go up that ramp," he says.   21

There are so many people! All the people wear blue and red.   33
They find their seats and sit down. Owen watches the game.   44

"Peanuts! Peanuts!" a woman yells.   49

Owen's father raises his hand. "We will have some peanuts,"   59
he says.   61

The woman hands Owen's father a big bag of peanuts. He   72
gives her money.   75

"Are you having fun?" Owen's father asks.   82

"Yes!" Owen says.   85

Directions Read the story to your child using a different voice for each character. Then ask your child to read it in the same way. Challenge your child to read without making mistakes.

Wrapping a Present

Kim's mother made a present. It is a book of pictures. The   12
pictures are for Kim's grandfather. The book is for his   22
birthday.   23

Kim's mother needs her help. "Can you bring me the   33
wrapping paper and ribbon?" she asks.   39

"Where are they?" Kim asks.   44

"They are in my closet. Please bring the red paper and   55
ribbon," Kim's mother says.   59

Kim goes to her mother's closet. There is a lot of wrapping   71
paper! She brings back the paper and ribbon.   79

"Thank you," Kim's mother says. "You can help tie the   89
ribbon!"   90

Directions Read the story "Wrapping a Present" to your child. Give each character a distinct voice. Then have your child practice reading the story in the same way.

School Dance

Duke woke up covered with pink spots. He had spots on his 12
face and legs. Could he go to the school dance? 22

"I itch!" said Duke. 26

"Those are very bad spots," said June. "Try not to 36
scratch them." 38

"All I can do is rub this itch," said Duke. "How will I dance?" 52

June went to the school dance. Duke stayed home. 61
Soon he felt better. 65

The next day, June said, "The dance was fun, 74
but I felt tired." 78

Then June had an itch. "Oh no!" she cried. "Do I have spots?" 91

"Yes, you have spots!" said Duke. "I hope you get better 102
before the next school dance!" 107

Directions Read "School Dance" to your child. Give Duke and June different voices. Then have your child practice reading the passage in the same way. Ask your child to read the entire passage without making mistakes.

Show and Tell

Mrs. Carter's class loves show and tell. On Friday, each child   11
brings in something to show. They sit in a circle and talk   23
about what they brought.   27

"I brought my stuffed dog, Roger," says Tamika. She shows   37
her friends the stuffed dog. "He is very special. My dad gave   49
him to me."   52

"I brought my favorite fire truck," says Joe. "It lights up and   64
makes noise when you push a button." Joe pushes the   74
button and the lights flash. The truck beeps.   82

"I brought a baseball. My dad took me to a game last week.   95
We got two players to sign the ball," says Tran. He shows   107
everyone the ball.   110

"Those are wonderful," says Mrs. Carter.   116

School + Home

Directions Read the story to your child. Allow the volume and pitch of your voice to rise and fall naturally. Use different voices for each character to bring the characters to life. Then ask your child to use different voices for each character as he or she practices reading the story.

Sam the Snowman

Anna and Ben looked at the deep, white snow. There would   11
be no school today. What should they do?   19

"We can build a snowman!" Anna said.   26

"Make your snowman soon because it will be sunny today!"   36
Mom called.   38

The children ran outside and jumped in the snow. They   48
made three big balls of snow and put them together. They   59
called their snowman Sam.   63

"Now we can put a red hat on Sam's head," said Ben.   75

Soon Anna and Ben went inside to eat lunch. "Good-bye,   85
Sam!" they called.   88

After lunch, the sun was bright. The snow was not very   99
deep. Sam was gone!   103

"Look! Sam's red hat is in the snow!" said Ben.   113

But where was Sam?   117

School + Home

Directions Read the story to your child in your normal speaking voice. Pay particular attention to using your voice expressively when reading dialogue or sentences ending in exclamation marks or question marks. Then ask your child to read the story without making any mistakes.

Name _____

At the Parade

Today Kobe's class will see a big parade. They are   10
very excited!   12

The children walk to the front of the school with their teacher   24
and wait for the parade to begin.   31

"Look!" Kobe says to Lin. "I can see five white horses!"   42

The horses hold their heads high as they march by. They   53
are very beautiful to watch. All the children clap.   62

Next come the funny clowns. They wear big hats. Some   72
clowns hold big red balls. Now the children laugh.   81

"Those clowns look so silly!" Lin says.   88

One clown jumps up and down. Another clown rides a pony.   99
The clowns smile and wave good-bye to the children.   108

"When is the next parade?" Lin and Kobe ask together.   118

Directions Read the story to your child in your normal speaking voice. Read the parts
of Kobe and Lin with expression in your voice to show how the characters might feel.
Then ask your child to read the story and match your speed and expression without
making mistakes.

What Can You See at the Park?

| Today Mrs. Kim's class is going to a park in the city. The | 13 |
| children are very excited about the trip. | 20 |

| "What will we do in the park?" Darnel asks Mrs. Kim. | 31 |

| "You will see many different trees, plants, and flowers," says | 41 |
| Mrs. Kim. "We can learn a lot there." | 49 |

| At the park, the class learned the names of different trees. "What is | 62 |
| the name of this tree?" asks Mrs. Kim. She points to a tall tree. | 76 |

| "It is a maple tree!" Darnel says. He points to another tree. "That | 89 |
| one is a pine tree!" he says. | 96 |

| The children draw pictures of the trees. Then they climb to the | 108 |
| top of a high hill. | 113 |

| "Look!" says Mrs. Kim, pointing. "We can see our school from here!" | 125 |

| The children eat lunch on the hill. There is so much to see! After | 139 |
| lunch, they look at flowers. | 144 |

| "I like these red flowers," Darnel says. "My mother grows those." | 155 |

| "I like them too," Mrs. Kim says. | 162 |

Directions Read the story "What Can You See at the Park?" to your child. As you read, your voice should rise and fall in a natural way. Give stress to important words. Then, with your child, take turns reading the story. After rereading a few times, ask your child to read the story with no mistakes.

Name _____

At the Pond

Marta and Hector will visit their grandmother today. Her   9
house is near a pond. A pond is a great place to visit. What   23
will Marta and Hector see there?   29

All morning, Marta and Hector laugh and race around the   39
pond. There are birds and animals there. They look in the   50
clear water. They see small fish swimming together.   58

"Why are the small fish swimming together?" Marta asks.   67

"The small fish want to stay safe," Grandmother says.   76
"Big fish also try to stay safe. They hide in the water."   88

"Look at the beautiful ducks swimming across the pond,"   97
Hector calls. He points at the ducks. "Why are their tails in   109
the air?"   111

"Those ducks turn upside down in the water to eat. Other   122
ducks swim under the water to find food," Grandmother   131
says. "Do you know what ducks eat?"   138

"Ducks eat plants. They also eat bugs," Marta and Hector   148
say. "We learned that at school. We learned about pond   158
plants and animals, too."   162

Directions Read the story "At the Pond" to your child. Your voice should rise and fall naturally. Give each character his or her own voice. Then ask your child to read the story in the same way. Challenge your child to read without mistakes.

Fluency Lesson 16   Expression/Intonation/Characterization 4   **95**

A Big Surprise!

All the children in Lavon's class are working hard! They are making   12
pictures for an art show at their school next Tuesday. They are also   25
making a special surprise for their teacher, Mrs. Cho.   34

"Painting a picture of my new puppy is fun!" says Lavon to his friend   48
Pam. "What are you drawing?"   53

"This is a raccoon. I saw one in the woods last summer," Pam says.   67

At the end of the day, the children hang up their art. Then Mrs. Cho   82
looks at all the pictures.   87

"Your pictures are beautiful. You all worked very hard," Mrs. Cho   98
says. "All your pictures will look wonderful at the art show."   109

"One of our pictures is not for the show," Lavon says happily.   121

Mrs. Cho looks surprised. "What is the picture for?" she asks.   132

The children hurry to the back of the classroom and hold up a big   146
birthday card. It is the special surprise they made for Mrs. Cho!   158

"Happy birthday, Mrs. Cho!" they all shout.   165

"Thank you!" says Mrs. Cho. She is so happy. She takes the card   178
and looks carefully at the pictures all the children drew. "This is   190
wonderful!"   191

Directions Read "A Big Surprise!" to your child. Use a different voice for each character. Then read the story again and take turns with your child reading different characters' words. Finally, ask your child to read the story alone and use a different voice for each character.

Name _____

The Pizza Project

Mrs. Ortiz gives her class a new project every month. This month they are   14

making lunch to thank their teachers. Mrs. Ortiz brings in all the food and   28

sets it up in the cafeteria. "I will show you how to make pizzas," she says.   44

The children all crowd around her to watch.   52

"First, you put the dough on a round pizza pan," she says. "Then you   66

spread a little sauce on the dough."   73

"How much sauce do you spread?" asks Erica.   81

"That's a good question!" Mrs. Ortiz says. "Fill up a big spoon about   94

four times. Then spread it around. Add more if there are any places   107

without sauce."   109

Mrs. Ortiz picks up a bowl of cheese. "Next, you take a handful of   123

cheese and spread it over the sauce. Make sure you cover all the sauce   137

with cheese."   139

"That looks really good!" Matt says.   145

"It will be," Mrs. Ortiz says. "Then you need to pick toppings. What   158

do we want to put on this pizza?"   166

"Pepperoni!" says Matt.   169

"Great," says Mrs. Ortiz. She puts the topping on the pizza. "Now it's   182

time to bake the pizza. I will take this into the kitchen while you all   197

put together your own pizzas."   202

Directions Read the story to your child. Allow the volume and pitch of your voice to rise and fall naturally. Use a voice for each child to bring the characters to life. Then ask your child to use a voice for each character as he or she practices reading the story.

Class Pet

Mr. Harris's class has a new pet! 7

Their new pet is a rabbit. Her name is Elsie. 17

Elsie has black fur and long ears. She is very soft. 28
Tyrone and Robin like to pet Elsie. 35

Elsie lives in her home called a hutch. She eats 45
leaves and rabbit food. She hops around the hutch. 54
She sleeps most of the day. 60

School + Home **Directions** Read the story to your child and pay attention to reading at a normal rate and using your voice expressively. Then ask your child to read the story without making any mistakes.

Father's Day

Alex wakes up very early. He is very excited!   9

Alex and his mother make breakfast. His mother makes   18
eggs and pancakes. Alex butters bread. His mother pours   27
a cup of coffee.   31

His mother puts the food on a tray. Alex picks up a card.   44
They go to his parents' room.   50

"Happy Father's Day!" Alex says.   55

Alex's father laughs. "Thank you, Alex," he says.   63

School + Home

Directions Read the story to your child in your normal speaking voice. Read the parts of Alex and Alex's father with expression in your voice to show how the characters might feel. Then ask your child to read the story and match your speed and expression without making any mistakes.

Kate Is Late

Mom called Kate. Kate slept very late, so she had to dress	12
fast. She cannot be late!	17

Nate helped Kate. He gave Kate a snack. Kate and Nate	28
packed fast. She is glad Nate helped. Kate must not be late!	40

Kate missed her bus. Will Mom take Kate? Yes, Mom can	51
take her. Kate will not be late!	58

Kate made it! She went to class. Then the class sang to her.	71
It was her birthday!	75

Directions Read the story "Kate Is Late" to your child. Use your normal voice and an unrushed manner. Then have your child practice reading it without making mistakes at the same speed he or she uses when talking.

School + Home

Bedtime

Eric had a very busy day.   6

He went to school. He played with his friends, Rob and Jack.   18
He walked his dog, cleaned his room, and ate dinner.   28

Then Eric took a shower. He sang in the shower. He read   40
books with his mother. Eric loves to read books. He likes to   52
read books about trucks.   56

Now it is time to go to bed! Eric's mother gives him a hug.   70
Then she turns out the light.   76

"Good night!" Eric says.   80

"Good night," his mother says.   85

School + Home

Directions Read the story "Bedtime" to your child. Your voice should rise and fall naturally. Emphasize important words. Then ask your child to read the story in the same way. Challenge your child to read without mistakes.

Five White Mice

Five white mice rode bikes. The mice rode up a hill. They made jokes to each other as they rode.

12
20

"This spot is nice. Let's stop here to eat," said one white mouse.

32
33

Five white mice sat on stones and ate cake. "This cake is delicious," said another white mouse. Five white mice did not see the brown kitten asleep nearby.

45
55
61

The brown kitten woke up and saw five white mice. Then the mice saw the kitten.

73
77

"It is time to go!" yelled five white mice. "Let's go home!"

89

Then five white mice ran to the five bikes. The five white mice rode and rode, and soon they were safe at home again.

101
112
113

School + Home **Directions** Read the story "Five White Mice" to your child, using your voice to show feeling. Then ask your child to practice reading it to you with expression.

Rex the Pest

Rex is the smallest dog on the block. Because he is small,　　12
he thinks the other dogs will pick on him.　　21

Boxer is the largest dog on the block. Every time Boxer　　32
walks by Rex's house, Rex makes sure to bark and growl　　43
at him. Finally, Boxer had enough.　　49

"Rex, why do you always bark at me? Do you not like me?"　　62
Boxer asks.　　64

"I just want to prove to you that I'm not afraid of you,"　　77
says Rex.　　79

"Why would you be afraid of me?" Boxer asks.　　88

"Because you're big, and I'm just a little dog," explains Rex.　　99

Boxer looks at Rex for a moment. "Rex, I've never been　　110
mean to you. In fact, I'd like to be friends if you'd let me,"　　124
Boxer says.　　126

Rex barks again. This time it's out of happiness.　　135
"Yes, I'll be your friend," says Rex.　　142

Directions Read the story "Rex the Pest" to your child at your normal rate of speaking.
Then ask your child to practice reading the passage without making mistakes.

Where Will Jin Go?

Dad had a big surprise for Jin's birthday.   8

"Tomorrow we will go to the new zoo," he said.   18

"Will I see big animals there?" asked Jin.   26

"Some animals are big, and some are small," Dad said.   36

The next day, Jin and Dad saw big brown bears at the zoo.   49
The bears played and splashed in the water. Dad and Jin   60
laughed.   61

"Can I see some small animals now?" Jin asked.   70

Then Dad and Jin saw the ducks and hens. Next, they visited   82
the baby goats and rabbits. Jin petted the goats and rabbits.   93
She even petted some horses and gave them food.   102

"What a great birthday gift!" Jin said. "When can we visit   113
the zoo again?"   116

Directions Read the story to your child with expression. Then ask your child to read it without making any mistakes. Remind your child to read in a way that sounds like he or she is talking to you.

Miniature Golf

Miniature golf is a very fun game. Each course has 18 holes.	12
Every hole is different. Some have little houses. Others have	22
hills or traps.	25
Amy, Damon, Lily, and Jason are going to play. Lily plays	36
all the time. Amy has never played.	43
They get their clubs and balls. Amy has a red ball. Lily has a	57
blue ball. Damon's ball is green, and Jason's ball is yellow.	68
They go to the first hole. Amy hits her ball first. The red ball	82
rolls down the green grass. It goes into the front door of the	95
little house.	97
The ball rolls out the back of the house. It rolls right into the	111
hole! Amy is very happy!	116

Directions Read the story to your child in your normal speaking voice. Read with excitement when you come to an exclamation mark. Then ask your child to read it and match your speed and expression without making any mistakes.

Name _____

Sick Day

Nat wakes up. He does not feel well. "Mom, I feel sick!" Nat says.   14

Mom touches Nat's cheek. "Oh, you are hot! You are sick.   25
You need to stay home from school," she says. Nat is sad.   37
He misses his friends. Nat lays on the couch. He watches   48
shows, and he reads books.   53

Mom makes soup for lunch. Nat loves soup. He likes to eat the   66
noodles Nat eats all the soup. Nat takes a nap. When he wakes up,   80
a bell is ringing. It is the doorbell. Who is here? David is here!   94

"Hello, David," says Nat.   98

"Hello, Nat. I brought your homework," David says.   106

"What did I miss?" Nat asks.   112

"We had a math test," David says. "Mr. Estrada says you can take it   126
when you feel better."   130

"Thank you," Nat says.   134

"Do you feel bad?" David asks.   140

"A little," Nat says. "Will you play a game with me?"   151

"Yes! What game should we play?" David asks.   159

"Let's play checkers," Nat says.   164

School + Home **Directions** Read the story "Sick Day" to your child. Give each character a distinct voice. Then have your child practice reading it the same way.

Fluency Lesson 18

Ellie Takes Pictures

Ellie loves to take pictures. She used to play with her mother's	12
old camera. Then she got her own camera. Ellie's camera is pink.	24
She keeps it in a bag. Ellie is careful with her camera.	36

Ellie takes a lot of pictures. She takes pictures of her friends,	48
her sister, and her dog Otto. Her sister Rachel likes to help Ellie.	61
They dress up Otto in old shirts. Then they take his picture. Otto	74
is a good dog. He is also a pretty dog.	84

Ellie goes to the zoo. She takes pictures of the lions. They have	97
pretty brown fur. She takes pictures of the flamingos. They are	108
pink, and they stand on one leg.	115

Ellie comes home. She takes pictures of her mother. Her	125
mother is cooking. Ellie's mother is making muffins.	133

Ellie stops taking pictures. "May I have a muffin?" she asks.	144

Ellie's mother laughs. "Yes, you may have a muffin,"	153
she says. Ellie sits down to eat.	160

Ellie's mother picks up the camera. "I will take a picture of	172
you!" she says.	175

Directions Read the story "Ellie Takes Pictures" to your child. Your voice should emphasize important words and show feeling. Then ask your child to read the story in the same way. Challenge your child to read without making mistakes.

A Lamb Named Happy

It is spring on the farm, and a lamb is just born. The farmer   14
and his daughter Cady name this new lamb Happy.   23

Soon Happy can run and play with the other lambs on the   35
farm. Cady helps her father by feeding the lambs and   45
putting straw in the barn.   50

"I like taking care of Happy," Cady says to her father. "When   62
he sees me, he sticks out his neck so I will pet him."   75

"Happy is a very smart lamb," says Father. "When his wool   86
gets thick and long, you can watch me cut it."   96

Cady helps her father take care of Happy for the next year.   108
When it is spring again, there are new lambs on the farm. It   121
is also time to cut Happy's wool. Cady's father will sell the   133
wool. Then other workers will make it into cloth.   142

"Will Happy feel very cold without all his long, thick wool?"   153
asks Cady.   155

"Our smart lamb will grow more wool soon," says Cady's   165
father with a big smile.   170

 Directions Read the story to your child in your normal speaking voice and at a normal speed. Read expressively to make the story interesting. Read the characters' words using different voices. Then have your child practice reading the story.

Name _____

Dinosaurs

What do you know about dinosaurs? Dinosaurs were amazing 9
animals. 10

Dinosaurs lived long, long ago. Scientists believe dinosaurs 18
lived millions of years ago. None are alive now. 27

Dinosaurs were reptiles. That means they were cold-blooded. 35
They had scales instead of skin. They laid eggs. There were 46
many kinds of dinosaurs. Some looked like birds without 55
feathers. They flew in the sky. Other dinosaurs swam in the 66
water. There were large and tiny dinosaurs. Some dinosaurs 75
ate meat, and others ate plants. 81

All the dinosaurs needed to protect themselves. Many used 90
their sharp teeth. Others had special ways to fight. Some 100
dinosaurs had sharp horns. Others had big hard plates of 110
bone on their backs or heads. Little dinosaurs usually would 120
hide or run away from danger. 126

The most famous kind of dinosaur is the Tyrannosaurus 135
Rex. It was more than 15 feet tall! It walked on two legs and 149
could run fast. It used its sharp teeth and claws to bite 161
smaller dinosaurs. It had tiny arms that probably didn't 170
help it catch food. The Tyrannosaurus lived in 178
North America. 180

 Directions Read the story "Dinosaurs" to your child. Read in a natural voice, as if you were talking to someone. Then ask your child to practice reading it to you the same way.

Name _____

Fred the Farmer

Fred the farmer feeds a cow.	6
Fred pets the cow.	10
Fred the farmer feeds a pig.	16
Fred pets the pig.	20
Fred the farmer feeds a dog.	26
Fred pets the dog.	30
Fred the farmer feeds a cow, a pig, and a dog.	41
Fred does his job.	45

School + Home **Directions** Have your child practice reading "Fred the Farmer" to you until he or she can read it without making any mistakes.

Fluency _____

The Big Race

Manny, Eddie, and Vince run a race!   7

Manny's brother Rico lines up the boys. "Ready?"   15
he asks. The boys nod. "Set!" he says. "Go!"   24

The boys run fast! They run down the sidewalk.   33
Manny is in front. Eddie is behind him. Vince   42
is last.   44

Then Vince catches up. Vince wins the race!   52

Directions Read the story to your child in your normal speaking voice. Read with excitement when you see an exclamation mark. Then ask your child to read the story and match your speed and expression without making any mistakes.

Gus Runs

Gus is a sad black pup. He wants to run. He wants to run,   14
hop, and trot! He wants to run in the grass and up the hills.   28

Gus slips past Dad. Gus runs and runs. He runs up hills. Hills   41
are fun! Gus runs, hops, and trots. Will he stop? No!   52

Gus sees a pond. Will he jump in? Yes! He swims, kicks,   64
and gets wet.   67

Gus smells snacks. Yum! Gus comes in. Gus licks Dad.   77
Thanks, Gus!   79

School + Home **Directions** Read the story "Gus Runs" to your child. Pay particular attention to reading each word correctly. Then ask your child to read it to you without making any mistakes.

A Surprise for Charlie

"Charlie, I have a surprise for you!" Charlie's mother said.   10

"What is it? Is it a dog? Are we going to visit Grandma?"   23
Charlie asked.   25

"No, but I think you will be happy. It is in the garage. Go   39
take a look," Charlie's mother said.   45

Charlie opened the door. He walked into the garage.   54

Charlie's father was there. He was standing in front of a   65
shiny red bike! "What do you think?" Charlie's father asked.   75

"Wow! Thank you, Dad!" Charlie said. "I will ride it now!"   86

School + Home

Directions Read the story "A Surprise for Charlie" to your child. Use your voice to make each character sound different. Then ask your child to read the story in the same way. Challenge your child to read without making mistakes.

Dog Show

Olivia loves dogs. She has four dogs: Shadow, Rocky,   9
Missy, and Ash. Olivia's dogs are all poodles. They   18
are big dogs with fuzzy black hair.   25

Olivia and her mother take Rocky to dog shows. Olivia's   35
mother gives Rocky a bath. Then she brushes his hair and   46
puts a leash on him. Rocky is a beautiful dog.   56

Olivia walks Rocky to the show ring. They wait with the   67
other dogs in their group. Then it is time to go.   78

Olivia and Rocky run around the show ring. The judge   88
looks at Rocky and checks his teeth. Rocky gets a treat!   99

The judge makes his decision. Rocky wins!   106

School + Home

Directions Read the story to your child in your normal speaking voice and at a normal speed. Read expressively to make the story interesting. Then have your child practice reading the story. Remind him or her to group words into phrases that make sense.

Horses

Horses are very interesting animals.   5

There are hundreds of different kinds of horses. The   14
smallest horses are miniature horses. They are about three   23
feet tall. Some of the largest horses are Clydesdales. They   33
can be six feet tall! Horses can be many colors, from white   45
to black. They can have spots or patches in different colors.   56

Mother horses give birth after about 11 months. Baby horses   66
can walk within hours of birth! Horses grow up in about four   78
years. They can live 25 to 30 years.   86

Horses begin training to carry riders when they are two to   97
four years old. People have been riding horses for about   107
6,000 years!   109

School + Home

Directions Read the story "Horses" to your child. Make your voice go up and down as if you were talking to someone. Then ask your child to practice reading it to you the same way.

The Country Mouse and the City Mouse

Once a Country Mouse lived happily in a little house on a   12
farm. "What a quiet home!" she thought.   19

Her friend lived in the city. "Please visit me!" the City Mouse   31
said. "We will have fun together in my big house."   41

So the Country Mouse visited the City Mouse. Inside the   51
house was a large table full of food. The mice jumped on the   64
table. They began to eat.   69

Then a big, hungry cat raced into the room.   78

The frightened mice jumped off the table. They hid under a   89
chair.   90

Then the Country Mouse packed her bags.   97

"Where are you going?" asked the City Mouse.   105

"I am going back to my nice, quiet home. I do not want to   119
see that cat again," said the Country Mouse.   127

And she never did.   131

Directions Read the story to your child at a normal speed. Let your voice rise and fall naturally. Give each mouse a different voice. Then take turns reading paragraphs. Finally, ask your child to read the story without making mistakes and using a different voice for each mouse.

Name _____

Loose Tooth

Henry has a loose tooth! At first, Henry is scared. He	11
does not want his tooth to fall out.	19
"Do not worry," Henry's mother says. "A new tooth	28
will grow in the same spot."	34
"Cool!" Henry says. "Will it hurt?"	40
"A little bit," Henry's mother says. "But you will get	50
a present when your tooth falls out."	57
"What do I get?" Henry asks.	63
"Put the tooth under your pillow at night. You will	73
see in the morning," Henry's mother says.	80
So Henry wiggles the tooth with his finger. He	89
wiggles it all day.	93
Henry wiggles it left. He wiggles it right. Then	102
it falls out!	105
Henry puts it under his pillow that night.	113
When he wakes up, Henry looks under his pillow.	122
There is a dollar!	126

School + Home

Directions Read the story to your child in your normal speaking voice. Give Henry and his mother each a distinct voice. Then ask your child to read the story and match your speed and expression without making any mistakes.

Patrick Goes to the Movies

Patrick likes to spend time with his Uncle Rob. They like to play   13
games and ride bikes together.   18

Today they are going to a movie. What movie should they see?   30
Patrick wants to see the movie about the dog. Uncle Rob picks   42
up Patrick in his car. They drive to the movies.   52

Uncle Rob buys tickets. Then they go inside.   60

"Would you like a snack?" Uncle Rob asks.   68

"Yes, please!" Patrick says.   72

Uncle Rob buys snacks. Uncle Rob and Patrick go into the theater.   84
They sit down right in the middle. Patrick's seat rocks.   94

Uncle Rob and Patrick eat snacks. They wait for the movie to start.   107
Then the lights turn off. The movie is starting! Patrick is happy.   119

In the movie, a dog is lost. The dog looks around. He cannot find   133
his owner. The dog goes on a long walk. He looks for his owner.   147

Patrick is sad. He wants the dog to find his owner. At the end,   161
the dog finds his owner. Patrick is happy.   169

After the movie, Patrick and Uncle Rob go home. They had a   181
good day!   183

School + Home **Directions** Read the story to your child. Pay particular attention to reading each word correctly and with expression. Then ask your child to read it to you without making any mistakes.

Lost in the Forest

One day two rabbits were hopping through the forest. These	10
rabbits were brothers. One rabbit was very small. His name was	21
Tiny. The other rabbit had a patch of white. His name was Patch.	34

As the brothers hopped along, the forest grew darker and darker.	45
Tiny stopped hopping. He looked around. The path was	54
hard to see. It did not look like the way home.	65

"Patch, I think we are lost," Tiny said.	73

Patch looked around. "Are you sure?" he asked. "I think home is	85
that way." Patch pointed.	89

Tiny shook his head. "No, it is that way," he said. He pointed	102
the other way.	105

"Where should we go?" Patch asked.	111

Leaves moved above them. "You should go that way," a voice said.	123

Patch and Tiny jumped. "Who said that?" Tiny asked.	132

"I did," the voice said. A squirrel ran down a tree and stood in the path.	148

"How do you know where we should go?" Patch asked.	158

The squirrel smiled. "That is easy! I can see your home from the	171
top of my tree."	175

"Oh! Thank you," said Tiny.	180

Directions Read the story "Lost in the Forest" to your child. Use your voice to make each character sound different. Then ask your child to read the story in the same way. Challenge your child to read without making mistakes.

Pluto

In 1930, Pluto was discovered. A scientist found Pluto by	10
looking through a telescope. A telescope can look at things	20
very far away. Pluto was named by an eleven-year-old girl.	32
Pluto is another name for Hades, a Greek god.	41

Pluto was called a planet. It is smaller than other planets, but	53
it is made of rock and moves around the Sun. Pluto is smaller	66
than the Moon! Pluto is often farther away from the Sun than	78
Neptune. It is very cold on Pluto. It is so cold that the air	92
freezes into ice.	95

Pluto is very hard to see, even with a telescope. No one	107
knows much about Pluto. A spaceship will reach Pluto in	117
2015 to take a closer look. Pluto does have a moon. The	129
moon is called Charon. It was discovered in 1978. Two	139
other tiny moons were found in 2005.	146

In 2006, scientists decided that Pluto was not a planet.	156
Pluto is now a dwarf planet. Dwarf planets are much smaller	167
than other planets. Most are very far from the Sun. One	178
dwarf planet, Ceres, is between Mars and Jupiter.	186

School + Home

Directions Read the story to your child in your normal speaking voice and at a normal speed. Read expressively to make the story interesting. Then have your child practice reading the story. Remind him or her to first read the story silently to become familiar with the words.

The Grand Canyon

Have you ever visited the Grand Canyon? It is a beautiful   11
place. The Grand Canyon is in Arizona. The canyon is one of   23
the deepest canyons on Earth! It is almost 300 miles long and   35
more than a mile deep in some places. It has forests and deserts.   48

The Colorado River made the Grand Canyon. Over millions   57
of years, the river wore away the rock. The river still runs   69
through the canyon.   72

The Grand Canyon is important to scientists, who study rocks.   82
There are many layers of rock in the canyon. The layers show   94
what the land was like long ago. They also show some of the   107
plants and animals that used to live there.   115

Native Americans have lived in the Grand Canyon for thousands   125
of years. In the 1500s, Spanish explorers visited the canyon.   135
In 1869, an Army major named John Wesley Powell explored the   146
canyon along the river.   150

By the early 1900s, people began going to the canyon on vacation.   162
In 1919, the Grand Canyon became a national park. Today, around   173
5 million people visit the Grand Canyon every year.   182

There is a lot to do there! People like to hike in the canyon. They ride   198
in boats on the river. They take tours. You can too!   209

Directions Read the story "The Grand Canyon" to your child. Make your voice go up
and down as if you were talking to someone. Then ask your child to practice reading it to
you the same way.